The Six-Minute Solution
A Reading Fluency Program (Primary Level)

Gail N. Adams, M.Ed.
Sheron M. Brown, M.A., M.S.

Grades K–2
and Remedial Grade 3

Published and Distributed by

Sopris West™
EDUCATIONAL SERVICES

A Cambium Learning Company

4093 Specialty Place • Longmont, Colorado 80504 • (303) 651-2829
www.sopriswest.com

128291\292\09-09

Acknowledgments

We would like to express our appreciation to:

Dr. Anita Archer, the most gifted teacher we have ever known. Her inspiration, friendship, and encouragement were instrumental in the development of this book.

Susan Van Zant and Teri Middleton, our dear friends and colleagues, for their willingness to assist us in writing and editing some of the material in this book.

Judy Wollberg of Sopris West, whose support and guidance were invaluable to us during this project.

Our immediate family members—Larry Adams, Jack Brown, and Jennifer Adams—for their patience, understanding, and love.

Our mothers—Ruth Novelli and Joan Miscall—who first instilled in us a love of reading.

Gail N. Adams
Sheron M. Brown

About the Authors

Gail N. Adams is a veteran teacher with 30 years of experience in elementary and middle schools. In addition to working as a resource specialist for the Poway (California) Unified School District, Adams served as an educational consultant for the San Diego Office of Education and the North County Professional Development Federation. As such, she was a contributing author and trainer for the materials developed under two California reading grants. Adams is also a nationally certified trainer for the *REWARDS, Effective Reading Intervention Academy, Summer Reading Camp*, and *Read Naturally* programs. She holds a master's degree in education with an emphasis in reading and is certified in general education, special education learning disabilities, and as a reading specialist.

Sheron M. Brown, a retired elementary reading specialist, was an educator for 38 years. She holds master's degrees in curriculum and instruction, reading, and educational administration. Brown began her teaching career in her home state of New Jersey and taught in Florida, Texas, Alaska, and California. She was a classroom teacher for grades 1–10 and an elementary administrator. Brown has also been an educational consultant for the San Diego County Office of Education and the North County Professional Development Federation. She conducts workshops and teacher trainings for school districts and conferences throughout the United States and is the author of four books of word-sorting and word-study activities: *All Sorts of Sorts, All Sorts of Sorts 2, All Sorts of Sorts 3*, and *Words They Need to Know* (with Sally Oppy). All are published by the Teaching Resource Center in San Diego, California.

Contents

Introduction

In order to become proficient readers, primary students must possess a foundational knowledge of phonetic elements, an automatic sight-word vocabulary, and the ability to read text fluently. The *Six-Minute Solution Primary* will help students do just that. Our research-based, effective instructional procedures are designed to "open the door to literacy" to primary students while using only six minutes of the instructional day.

The program contains assessments, instructional formats, and fluency practice sheets for common phonetic elements; as well as automatic words lists and nonfiction reading passages that are designed for partner practice, but can also be implemented with small instructional groups or individual students. Teachers may choose to introduce the *Six-Minute Solution Primary* activities in one of two ways: (1) they may follow the general description of the activity; or (2) they may follow the scripted format for the activity, which provides exact wording to use when introducing the concepts.

Phonetic Elements

The explicit teaching of sounds (phonemes) and the letters used to represent them (graphemes) is known as *systematic phonics instruction*. According to a report of the National Reading Panel (National Institute of Child Health and Human Development; NICHD, 2000), "Systematic phonics instruction produces gains in reading and spelling, not only in the early grades (K–2) but also in the later grades (2–6), and among children having difficulty learning to read."

Phonetic Elements Fluency Building Sheets (see *Fluency Building Sheets*) are designed to build fluency at the individual letter, sound, and decodable word level. There are 113 skills sheets included in this section. *Decodable Short-Vowel and Long-Vowel Stories* (also found in *Fluency Building Sheets*), which focus on targeted phonetic elements, are provided for additional reinforcement. There are a total of 20 stories—ten focusing on short-vowel words, and ten focusing on long-vowel words—in this section.

Automatic Words

Automatic words are those that occur with high frequency in textbooks for grades 1–8. Since these words repeatedly appear—a mere 13 words account for more than 25% of the words in print (Johns & Lenski, 2001)—it is imperative that primary students be able to read these words automatically. The 25 *Automatic Words Fluency Building Sheets* (see *Fluency Building Sheets*) are designed to build fluency at the sight-word level by having students read and reread the same ten words on each list until they can read them at a rate of one word per second, or 60 correct words per minute (cwpm).

Practice Passages

The 75 *Practice Passages* (see *Fluency Building Sheets*) are based on social studies and science standards. The passages are broken down by grade level—1, 2, and 3—and each grade level has five different themed units, each containing five related passages with common vocabulary. The five passages in each themed unit are sequenced in successively higher reading levels within that grade. As students practice fluency by reading the *Practice Passages*, they also enhance their background knowledge and content-area vocabulary.

Rereading to Build Fluency

As the saying goes, "Practice makes perfect," whether it's shooting basket-balls, playing the piano, or processing text in a smooth, efficient, and accurate manner. The benefits of repeated readings of the same passage to build reading fluency have been well documented in many research studies (Levy, Nicholls, & Kroshen, 1993; Meyer & Felton, 1999; Samuels, 1979). The *Six-Minute Solution Primary* helps students succeed at reading fluency by using an instructional model that is based on repeated-reading research and partnering students whose instructional and fluency levels most closely match (see *Table I.1*). Research supports the fact that students' reading skills improve when they work with peers in structured reading activities (Greenwood, Delquadri, & Hall, 1989; Rosenshine & Meister, 1994; Stevens, Madden, Slavin, & Famish, 1987).

Table I.1		
THE *SIX-MINUTE SOLUTION PRIMARY* INSTRUCTIONAL FORMAT		
Time	**Materials**	**Procedures**
1 minute	■ Two copies of the same *Fluency Building Sheet* or *Practice Passage* in plastic sleeves. ■ One dry-erase marker and an erasing cloth in a zipper-lock plastic bag. ■ Two *Fluency Record* sheets. ■ A digital timer or stopwatch.	■ Teacher announces that fluency timings will begin. ■ Teacher hands out materials to student partners. ■ Students remove fluency materials from their partnership's portfolio. ■ Partners record today's date on their respective *Fluency Record* sheets. Partner 1 will read first; Partner 2 will highlight Partner 1's errors and stopping point with the dry-erase marker on the transparent plastic sleeve. ■ Teacher monitors to ensure students are ready to begin their timings.
1 minute		■ Teacher sets timer and says, "Begin." ■ All Partner 1s read. ■ All Partner 2s mark Partner 1 reading errors and stopping point on his/her copy of the *Fluency Building Sheet* or *Practice Passage*.
1 minute		■ All Partner 2s give feedback. ■ Partner 2 tells Partner 1 how many elements/words he/she read, the number of errors he/she made, and does the error-correction procedure. ■ Partner 1 records the numbers on his *Fluency Record* sheet. ■ Partner 2 wipes off the dry-erase markings on his fluency builder and gives the dry-erase marker to Partner 1.
1 minute		■ All Partner 2s read. ■ Teacher again sets timer and says, "Begin." ■ Partner 2 reads the same *Fluency Building Sheet* or *Practice Passage* to Partner 1. Partner 1 marks Partner 2 errors and records the stopping point on his/her copy of the fluency builder.

1 minute		■ All Partner 1s give feedback. ■ Partner 1 tells Partner 2 how many words he/she read, how many errors he/she made, and does the error-correction procedure. ■ Partner 2 records the numbers on his *Fluency Record* sheet. ■ Partner 1 wipes off the dry-erase markings on his fluency builder and returns the dry-erase marker and erasing cloth to the zipper-lock plastic bag.
1 minute		■ Students put materials away. ■ Students return their *Fluency Building Sheet* or *Practice Passage*, *Fluency Record* sheets, and zipper-lock plastic bags with the dry-erase marker and erasing cloth to their portfolios.

Six-Minute Solution Primary Sample Schedule

Monday
- All partnerships have new fluency building sheets or passages. Partners preview the entire fluency sheet or passage for accuracy (i.e., whisper-read or silently read, underlining unknown words). Teacher monitors and identifies any unknown words to either partner.
  Option 1: No timings on Mondays. Have partners use the allotted six minutes for previewing passages.
  Option 2: Allow extra time (10–15 minutes) on Mondays. Have partners first preview their fluency building sheet or passage for accuracy. Then, conduct partner fluency practice during the allotted six minutes.

Tuesday through Thursday
- The *Six-Minute Solution Primary* procedure: Fluency practice.

Friday
- Partners turn in their fluency building sheet or passage and select new ones.
  Option for *Practice Passages*: Extend the amount of time on Fridays to incorporate comprehension strategies or summary writing. Have students use the practiced passage before turning it in and selecting a new one. See *Chapter 8* for comprehension and writing strategies suggestions.

Partnering Students to Build Fluency

In the *Six-Minute Solution Primary*, students' current instructional reading levels are determined, and then students are placed in fluency partnerships. In these partnerships, one student reads the passage or fluency building sheet to his/her partner for one minute while the partner tracks the words read correctly as well as the reading errors. The partners then switch roles, with each partner charting his or her own progress. The entire procedure takes only six minutes.

Decoding & Fluency

Experts may disagree as to what exactly is the best approach to teach students how to read, but they are in agreement as to what good reading "sounds" like. According to Carnine, Silbert, and Kame'enui (1997), *fluency* is "reading smoothly, easily, and quickly." In order to read fluently, the reader must be able to decode the vast majority of words automatically, with approximately 95% accuracy. However, although there is a clear link between fluency and decoding skills, fluency practice alone will not improve a student's decoding skills. Any underlying decoding problems must also be addressed either prior to or in conjunction with fluency practice.

Comprehension & Fluency

Research also shows a high correlation between reading *comprehension* and reading *fluency* (Farstrup & Samuels, 2002; Foorman & Mehta, 2002; LaBerge & Samuels, 1974). If a student is focusing his/her cognitive energies on word decoding and recognition, those energies are not available for comprehension. In the words of Farstrup and Samuels (2002), *fluency* consists of "optical, perceptual, syntactic, and semantic cycles, each melting into the next as readers try to get meaning as efficiently as possible using minimal time and energy."

Independent Reading & Fluency

Fluent readers generally find reading to be a pleasurable activity; as a result, they read more. When the amount of time spent on independent reading increases, there are accompanying gains in reading-related skills. As students read more, they increase not only their comprehension but also their vocabulary, background knowledge, decoding, and fluency skills. The "Matthew effect"—a term coined by reading researcher Dr. Keith Stanovich—refers to the effect that in reading, as in other areas of life, "the rich get richer while the poor get poorer" (Stanovich, 1986).

Work Completion & Fluency

Fluent readers will be better able to complete both class assignments and homework. As an example, consider two students reading at the second-grade level. Student A—a fluent second-grade reader—is able to read an average of 80 cwpm. Student B—a struggling second-grade reader—has an average fluency rate of 20 cwpm. Both students are assigned the same amount of reading. Student A, with an appropriate fluency rate, is able to complete the reading assignment in 20 minutes. Student B, who reads four times slower than Student A, needs more than an hour to complete the same assignment.

Reading Achievement & Fluency Practice

Although the National Assessment of Educational Progress (Pinnell, Piluski, Wixson, Campbell, Gough, & Beatty, 1995) found that 44% of fourth graders were not fluent readers, research shows that educators have the knowledge and tools to positively affect this problem. After analyzing many fluency studies, the National Reading Panel (NICHD, 2000) reported that fluency can be taught and that guided, repeated, oral-reading procedures are "appropriate and valuable avenues for increasing reading fluency and overall reading achievement." Skilled readers read words quickly, correctly, and without hesitation. Students who have not become fluent readers continue to plod slowly through each sentence without experiencing the joy of quick, automatic, fluent reading. By its very nature, fluency practice supports comprehension. It provides a skill-building activity that enables students to move quickly through text. As students build fluency through rereading, they amass a larger reading vocabulary. As they begin to read with automaticity, their cognitive attention can be focused on the text's meaning instead of on word identification. The National Reading Panel (NICHD, 2000) found that repeated oral reading, accompanied by feedback and guidance, resulted in significant reading achievement.

The *Six-Minute Solution Primary* uses both of these research-validated components—repeated readings of the same passage and/or fluency building sheet as well as oral feedback from peers—to build reading fluency.

Program Overview

The *Six-Minute Solution Primary* is based on the premise that six minutes' worth of concentrated practice on targeted literacy skills—such as phonetic elements, automatic words recognition, and passage reading—can increase student reading achievement. The program can be easily implemented in a variety of educational settings by following six easy steps, each of which are discussed in the first six chapters.

Chapter 1: Assessments

Assessment is critical for determining individual student needs, forming student partnerships, and grouping students. The assessments found in this program include:

- Letter recognition
- Letter/sound correspondence
- Phonetic elements (e.g., short and long vowels, CVC, CVCC, CVC**e** patterns)
- Automatic words
- Placement passages

Chapter 2: Selecting Fluency Partners and Instructional Groupings

This chapter provides suggestions for forming student partnerships and instructional groups for the purpose of fluency building.

Chapter 3: Introducing the Fluency Concept

This chapter provides the necessary steps for introducing to students the concept of repeated practice.

Chapter 4: Establishing Partner Behavior

Suggestions are offered for training students how to:

- Be supportive partners
- Work in a cooperative manner
- Provide polite feedback

Chapter 5: Training Students in the Partnership Model

Chapter 5 provides step-by-step instructions to train students in the partnership model. It also includes adaptations for individualized and small-group practice.

Chapter 6: Managing Materials

Well-organized materials that are easily accessible to students will assist in the establishment of effective fluency routines. Tips for materials management as well as for monitoring student progress and making instructional decisions based on student progress are included in this chapter.

Chapter 7: Student Progress and Record Keeping

It is essential to monitor student progress and make instructional decisions based on individual student progress. Chapter 7 provides examples of how to interpret fluency data, adjust student goals, and support students who are not making adequate progress.

Chapter 8: Comprehension and Writing Strategies

The fluency passages contained in this program may also be used to support comprehension and writing strategies. Chapter 8 offers suggestions for teaching students how to summarize, paraphrase, retell, describe, sequence, compare, problem-solve, and determine cause and effect. The passages may also be used to teach students to write a short summary. Examples of paragraph frames are included.

Chapter 9: Building Letter/Sound Fluency

Letter-naming fluency in kindergarten is a strong predictor of future reading achievement. Chapter 9 provides information, instructional strategies, and teaching procedures to increase students' automatic letter-identification ability as well as sound-symbol correspondence.

Chapter 10: Building Phonetic Elements Fluency

Phonics, an understanding of the relationship between the letters of a written language and the corresponding sounds of its spoken language, is a vital reading skill. This chapter contains the continuum of phonetic elements presented in one-minute practice and fluency formats designed to build automatic recognition of these essential reading elements.

Chapter 11: Building Automatic Words Fluency

An automatic sight-word vocabulary is a critical literacy skill. Chapter 11 provides instructional formats and teaching procedures to help build automatic word fluency.

Conclusion: More Than Six Minutes a Day

With the *Six-Minute Solution Primary* partnership model, students are able to increase their phonetic element, automatic word, and/or passage reading fluency by practicing for only six minutes a day on a regular basis. There will be times, however, when teachers will need to devote more than six minutes a day to fluency practice. The *Conclusion* outlines some situations that may require extended practice.

CHAPTER 1

Assessments

The first step in implementing the *Six-Minute Solution Primary* is to determine students': (1) knowledge of phonetic elements; (2) level of sight-word acquisition; (3) oral reading rate on a grade-level passage; and (4) instructional reading level. Three different assessments are included in the *Six-Minute Solution Primary*:

- Phonetic Elements Assessment
- Automatic Words Assessment
- Passage Reading Assessment (includes oral reading fluency/instructional reading level)

All three assessments do not need to be given in order to use the program. Depending on a student's instructional level, the teacher may elect to focus on fluency building for phonetic elements and/or sight-word fluency before passage reading fluency. More proficient readers may need to work only on passage reading fluency. Teachers should also consider *DIBELS* (Good & Kaminski, 2003) or other diagnostic assessments in determining the appropriate fluency building entry point for their students.

We recommend that students be assessed for fluency a minimum of three times a year (fall, winter, and spring) for progress monitoring purposes. Placement passages can be used for this purpose as identified later in this chapter.

Students who have significant reading problems may need a more extensive assessment than is described in this program in order to determine the nature and severity of their reading problems. The more extensive assessment information can either replace the *Six-Minute Solution Primary* assessments or be used in conjunction with them.

Phonetic Elements Assessment

This assessment measures mastery of individual letter names and sounds, single-syllable short-vowel words, single-syllable long-vowel words, consonant blends and digraphs, vowel combinations, and "**r**"-controlled vowels. There are six subtests in the *Phonetic Elements Assessment*. Each subtest consists of a Student Copy, a Teacher Record Sheet for documenting individual student scores, and a Class Record Sheet. Teachers should select the appropriate subtest for each student based on the best estimate of student knowledge. For example, a kindergarten teacher might select the Letters and Sounds subtest at the beginning of the school year, while a first-grade teacher might select the CVC Short Vowel Patterns subtest at the same point in time.

Materials:
- Two copies of the Student Copy of the selected subtest—one for the student and one for the examiner—laminated or enclosed in a plastic sleeve.
- One copy of the Teacher Record Sheet of the selected subtest on which the teacher marks a student's errors and stopping point.
- A marking pen and a highlighter for the teacher.

Estimated Time:
2–5 minutes per student, depending on how many subtests are administered.

Activity Procedure:
1. Hand the student a Student Copy of the selected subtest.
2. Instruct the student to say the letter name, the letter sound, or the word, depending on the subtest being administered. Allow no more than 3 seconds per subtest item before marking the item as incorrect.
3. As the student responds, follow along and track the correct responses as well as the errors.
4. Continue administering the subtests until the student's accuracy rate drops below 90%.

Notes:
- Assessments should be administered individually and out of hearing distance of other students.
- Noting correct responses in a different pen color at each point in the school year (e.g., red for fall, blue for winter, green for spring) provides a visual representation of a student's progress over time.
- A Class Record Sheet is included within each phonetic element subtest. Listing all students and their scores on the Class Record Sheet aids teachers in forming instructional groups.
- An Individual Comprehensive Phonetic Element Assessment form on which to record a student's scores from the six subtests is included at the end of the *Phonetic Elements Assessment* section.
- Individual subtests may also be used for progress monitoring purposes.

Automatic Words Assessment

This assessment contains lists of the most frequently encountered sight words in reading texts (Carroll, Davies, & Richman, 1971). There are 25 subtests (lists) in this assessment. Each list contains ten sight words ranging in order of frequency, from most frequent to least frequent. Teachers should select the appropriate list for each student based on their best estimate of student knowledge.

Materials:
- Two copies of the Student Copy of the selected word list(s)—one for the student and one for the examiner—laminated or enclosed in a plastic sleeve.
- One copy of the Teacher Record Sheet for each student being assessed.
- A marking pen and a highlighter for the teacher.

Estimated Time:
2.5 minutes per student, depending on how many lists are administered.

Activity Procedure:
1. Hand the student a Student Copy of the selected word list(s).
2. Instruct the student to read the words quickly and carefully.

3. Follow along, drawing a line through any word the student does not read correctly **within three seconds**, and record errors at the bottom of the word list(s).
4. When a student misses one word on any list, stop. This is the list number that the student should begin practicing.
5. A Class Record Sheet is included at the end of the *Automatic Words Assessment.* Listing all students and their individual instructional-level list number on the Class Record Sheet aids teachers in forming instructional groups.

Passage Reading Assessment

The primary purpose of this assessment is to obtain both an oral reading rate and an instructional reading level for each student in order to pair reading partners. The results of this assessment provide baseline information so that student growth can be evaluated. The two subtests in this assessment include Oral Reading Fluency and Instructional Reading Level.

Oral Reading Fluency Assessment

Oral reading fluency is the number of correct words per minute (cwpm) a student reads on a grade-level passage. To determine a student's individual oral reading fluency, the teacher listens to the student read a grade-level passage aloud for one minute, noting the total number of words read and subtracting any errors to obtain the cwpm score. For the purpose of assessment, students must read a passage appropriate for their grade level (e.g., second-grade students must read a second-grade passage). Teachers may use one of the *Assessment Passages* (see *Assessments*) included in the *Six-Minute Solution Primary* or a grade-level fluency passage of their choice. **Note:** While students must read a grade-level passage for the purpose of assessment, they should be assigned passages at their individual instructional reading level.

Materials:

- Two copies of an *Assessment Passage* (see *Assessments*) at the student's grade level—one for the student to read from and one for the teacher to record reading errors and the stopping point—laminated or enclosed in a plastic sleeve. Each student in the class will read the same passage individually (e.g., all first-grade students will read the same Level 1 *Assessment Passage*).
  Note: When listening to an individual student read, sit apart from the other students so that they are not within hearing distance. This would give them prior knowledge of the passage.
  Note: The teacher may wish to have one copy of the same *Placement Passage* for each student on which to permanently record reading errors and the stopping point. In that case, the teacher will need as many copies of the *Assessment Passage* as there are students in the class.
- One copy of the *Initial Assessment Record* (see *Appendix*) on which to record all students' cwpm scores.
- A digital timer or stopwatch, a marking pen, and a clipboard.
  Special circumstances: When working with groups of students who read significantly below grade level, it would not be appropriate to ask

them to read a grade-level *Assessment Passage*. Instead, assess remedial students with a *Assessment Passage* at their estimated reading levels. Continue assessing to determine the level at which a student reads with 95% accuracy (e.g., five errors in a 100-word passage). This would be the appropriate level for a student to begin building fluency.

Activity Procedure:

1. Give each student a laminated copy of the *Assessment Passage* and say, "The title of this passage is _____. When I say 'Please begin,' I would like you to start reading here (point to the first word) and read out loud quickly and carefully until the timer sounds. If you do not know a word, I will tell it to you. Are you ready?"
2. Set the timer for one minute and say, " I will start the timer when you begin reading."
3. Using a clipboard to hold the teacher copy of the *Assessment Passage*, follow along as the student reads, underlining errors. Mark a diagonal line when the timer sounds, indicating the point at which the student stopped reading. The use of the clipboard will keep the student from being distracted by any marks the teacher may make.
4. Tell the student, "Thank you. Please return to your seat and ask _____ (the next student) to come over to read."
5. During the interval between students, determine the total number of words the student read, subtract any errors, and note the cwpm read.
6. When all students have read the *Assessment Passage*, record their scores on the *Initial Assessment Record*.

Oral Reading Errors:

- Mispronunciations, unless attributed to accent or dialect.
- Words supplied by the teacher.
- Word omissions.
- Dropped word endings, unless attributed to accent or dialect.
- Substitutions, even if the word meaning is unchanged (e.g., "home" for "house").
- Reversed order of words counts as two errors (e.g., "he was" for "was he").

Notes:

- Repetitions are not counted as errors (e.g., "the boy, the boy").
- Insertions do not count as errors or as words read.
- Mispronunciations of proper nouns count as one error every occurrence.

Instructional Reading Level Assessment

A variety of assessments can be used to obtain a close approximation of a primary student's instructional reading level. These include word recognition tests and silent reading tests. Informal reading inventories can also be used. Teachers should select the type of assessment that best suits their needs.

Word Recognition Test
Materials:

- *San Diego Quick Assessment of Reading Ability* (see *Assessments*).

Estimated Time:
About 2 minutes per student.

Activity Procedure:
1. Make copies of the Student Form, Teacher Record, and scoring sheet.
2. Administer the test per the directions in the introductory paragraph.
3. Transfer student scores to the scoring sheet.

Silent Reading Test

Teachers of students who read at grade 2 level or above may choose to use a silent reading test to obtain students' instructional reading level. The advantage of using a group silent reading test is that it can be administered to all students at the same time. While students are taking the test, the teacher can read with individual students to obtain an oral reading fluency rate.

Materials:
- Copies of the test for all students in the class.

Estimated Time:
Will vary, depending on the test.

Activity Procedure:
1. Choose a silent reading test that can be administered to the entire class during one class period. Examples of commercially prepared tests, which lend themselves well to this procedure, include:
    a. Scholastic Reading Inventory (SRI) (Scholastic, Inc., 2003). Scores are reported in Lexile levels.
    b. Gates-MacGinitie Reading Tests (MacGinitie, MacGinitie, Maria, & Dreyer, 2003). Scores are reported in percentiles.
    c. McLeod Test of Reading Comprehension (Consortium on Reading Excellence; CORE, 1999). Scores are reported in grade-level scores.
    d. Measures of Academic Progress (MAPs). Scores are reported in RIT (Rasch Unit) scores, which use individual-item difficulty values to estimate student achievement.
2. Explain the test directions to the class and complete practice items with students.
3. Instruct students to begin working on the silent reading test. Make sure that students have something they can do independently when they finish the test.
4. After all of the students are finished, record their scores.
Special circumstances: Students who are enrolled in Title 1, remedial reading, special education, or English Language Learner (ELL) classes, or who have significant reading problems may be more appropriately assessed with an individually administered reading test such as the Woodcock Reading Mastery Test (Woodcock, 2000).

Using the *Assessment Passages* to Monitor Progress and Make Instructional Decisions

In addition to using the *Assessment Passages* to determine oral reading fluency, the passages may also be used to monitor progress and make instructional decisions:

- To measure student progress after several weeks of daily fluency practice, select the same *Assessment Passage* as utilized for the original baseline data collection. Have the initial fluency scores that were recorded on the *Initial Assessment Record* available for comparison.
- Conduct the one-minute timing assessment and calculate the student's cwpm score. Subtract the original cwpm score from the present number to determine the number of words gained per minute resulting from the fluency practice.
- Share the increase of words gained per minute with the student and the student's parents by illustrating the gain on the *Parent Fluency Assessment Report* (see *Appendix*).
- As students reach the reading fluency benchmark for their instructional level passages, move on to the *Assessment Passage* at the next instructional level and conduct an unpracticed fluency assessment.
- Use *Table 1.1* (Hasbrouck & Tindal, 2005) to determine if a student's instructional reading level has increased. If so, assign *Practice Passages* at the new level.

Appropriate Fluency Rate

Refer to *Table 1.1* (Hasbrouck & Tindal, 2005) for oral reading fluency rates by grade and season of the year. As a general rule, any student who scores below 50% on grade-level passages would benefit from a fluency-building program. Since it is recommended that students practice fluency building on instructional-level passages, their target fluency rate should be based on the instructional reading level. For example, the fluency goal for a second-grade student reading at mid first-grade level would be based on the first-grade, not the second-grade norms.

Table 1.1
2005 Hasbrouck & Tindal Oral Reading Fluency Data

Jan Hasbrouck and Gerald Tindal completed an extensive study of oral reading fluency in 2004. The results of their study are published in a technical report entitled, "Oral Reading Fluency: 90 Years of Measurement," which is available on the University of Oregon's website, **brt.uoregon.edu/tech_reports.htm.**

The table below shows the mean oral reading fluency of students in grades 1 through 8 as determined by Hasbrouck and Tindal's data.

You can use the information in this table to draw conclusions and make decisions about the oral reading fluency of your students. **Students scoring below the 50th percentile using the average score of two unpracticed readings from grade-level materials need a fluency-building program.** In addition, teachers can use the table to set the long-term fluency goals for their struggling readers.

Note that there is a difference between monitoring and placement. **Monitoring** with an assessment tool such as *Reading Fluency Monitor* can help you identify students who need to improve their fluency and monitor their progress over time.

Placement is the process of selecting an appropriate level of reading material and setting a reading rate goal within the context of a fluency-building program, such as READ NATURALLY. To place students in READ NATURALLY, use the READ NATURALLY placement table.

Grade	Percentile	Fall cwpm*	Winter cwpm*	Spring cwpm*
3	90	128	146	162
	75	99	120	137
	50	71	92	107
	25	44	62	78
	10	21	36	48
4	90	145	166	180
	75	119	139	152
	50	94	112	123
	25	68	87	98
	10	45	61	72
5	90	166	182	194
	75	139	156	168
	50	110	127	139
	25	85	99	109
	10	61	74	83
6	90	177	195	204
	75	153	167	177
	50	127	140	150
	25	98	111	122
	10	68	82	93
7	90	180	192	202
	75	156	165	177
	50	128	136	150
	25	102	109	123
	10	79	88	98
8	90	185	199	199
	75	161	173	177
	50	133	146	151
	25	106	115	124
	10	77	84	97

Grade	Percentile	Fall cwpm*	Winter cwpm*	Spring cwpm*
1	90		81	111
	75		47	82
	50		23	53
	25		12	28
	10		6	15
2	90	106	125	142
	75	79	100	117
	50	51	72	89
	25	25	42	61
	10	11	18	31

*cwpm = Correct Words Per Minute

CHAPTER 2

Selecting Fluency Partners and Instructional Groupings

When selecting fluency partners, an appropriate match is critical to their individual and collective success. Partner students as closely as possible by both oral reading fluency rates and instructional reading levels. An example of an appropriate match is a partnership between two third-grade students whose shared instructional reading level is grade 1 and whose oral fluency rates are within ten words of each other. If one of these third-grade students had an oral reading fluency rate of 45 cwpm and the other had an oral reading fluency rate of 65 cwpm, they would be mismatched as fluency partners. The slower-reading student would not be able to follow along with his partner's more rapid rate of reading.

Keeping in mind that student partners must always read the same *Practice Passage*, you could partner a third-grade ELL student reading at the second-grade level with a third-grade special education student who is also reading at the second-grade level.

Occasionally, there may be an "outlying" student—one whose instructional reading level does not match that of any other student. This student may be partnered with a teacher, an aide, or a classroom volunteer. Fluency partners can be selected by using spreadsheet software or by manually sorting students' oral reading fluency rates and instructional reading-level scores using graphs and records included in the *Appendix* section of this book.

Using Spreadsheets to Select Fluency Partners

For large groups of students, the easiest way to select fluency partners is to use spreadsheet software. The following steps will help you create the spreadsheet:

1. Begin by opening a new document (blank spreadsheet) and naming it (e.g., Language Arts Period 3, Mr. Smith's Third-Grade Class).
2. Label six columns with the following headings: Last Name, First Name, Date, Grade, Oral Reading Fluency Rate (cwpm), and Instructional Reading Level.
3. Enter the data in the six columns for each student.
4. Sort the data first by fluency (cwpm) and then by instructional reading level, in either ascending or descending order.
5. Assign fluency partners based on the sort (e.g., the first two students on the list would be partners, the second two students would be partners, and so on).

Manually Sorting Scores to Select Fluency Partners

Another method you can use to select fluency partners is to manually rank students. The following steps will help you sort your students' scores more easily:

1. Sort your students' Oral Reading Fluency Assessment (see *Chapter 1*) scores in ascending order (from lowest to highest).
2. In the first column on the Initial Assessment Record (see *Appendix*), list students in the order of their oral-reading fluency scores.
3. In the second column, list the oral-reading fluency score for each student.

4. In the third column list the students' instructional reading-level scores—from the San Diego Quick Assessment of Reading Ability (see *Assessments*) or another reading test.
5. Match students as closely as possible based on the data, making sure that each partnership's fluency score is within ten words of one another and both students are reading at the same instructional level.

Selecting Instructional Groupings

The *Six-Minute Solution Primary* is fundamentally designed for an entire classroom, but the following grouping configurations can also be used successfully:

- Small groups within a class
- Cross-age partnerships
- Parent-student partnerships
- Individual fluency programs

Entire Classroom

In this instructional grouping, the entire classroom is assessed and fluency partnerships are assigned. All Partner 1s read the assigned *Practice Passage* to their partners for one minute. While they are reading, Partner 2s mark Partner 1 errors and stopping points on their own laminated copy of the passage. Partner 1s then record their own final score (cwpm) on their *Fluency Record* (see *Appendix*). All Partner 2s then read the same *Practice Passage* for one minute. Results are tracked by Partner 1s on their laminated copy of the passage. Partner 2s then record their own final score (cwpm) on their *Fluency Record*. When fluency practice is completed for the day, partners store their portfolios, which contain the laminated *Practice Passages*, *Fluency Records*, and a zipper-lock plastic bag with a dry-erase marker and erasing cloth.

Small Groups Within a Class

Repeated reading practice can also be implemented in a small-group setting—such as within a guided reading group—using the same passage for students reading at the same instructional level. A sample schedule is as follows:

Monday

- The teacher and students preview passages for accuracy. The teacher sets a timer for one minute. Students whisper-read to themselves.
- When the timer sounds, students calculate the cwpm they read and graph the number on their *Fluency Record*. This is their initial reading score.

Tuesday, Wednesday, Thursday

- The teacher and students choral-read the passage together for one minute.
- The teacher then sets a timer for one minute. Students whisper-read the passage to themselves.
- When the timer sounds, students calculate their cwpm and graph the number on their *Fluency Record*.

Friday
- Final timing, using one of two options:

  Option 1—Students pair up. Teacher sets a timer for one minute. One student reads while the partner follows along, underlining any word errors and circling the last word read. Partner tells the reader how many cwpm were read, and the reader records the number on his/her *Fluency Record*. This is the final timing. The teacher then resets the timer for another minute. Students repeat the process, with roles reversed.

  Option 2—The teacher listens to each student read for one minute while the other students follow along silently. The teacher tells each student his/her cwpm read on the final timing. Students graph their own results.

Cross-Age Partnerships

Many elementary schools pair older classes with primary classes in a "big buddy" setting. The older students conduct one-minute fluency timings and record the data of their younger "buddies." After fluency timings have been conducted, the older and younger students then take part in whatever other "buddy" activities the teacher has decided for them.

Parent-Student Partnerships

A very effective way of engaging families in their children's fluency progress and provide additional fluency practice is by having them use the appropriate *Fluency Building Sheets* with their children. Drilling students with *Automatic Words Fluency Building Sheets* and *Grade-Level Practice Passages* (see *Reproducibles*) are very effective ways of engaging families in their children's fluency progress. Parents can be trained to conduct one-minute fluency timings and to record data either at school or at home. Students can bring the home recording sheets to school and have them checked by the teacher. Additional *Fluency Building Sheets* can be sent home based on the recorded data. As parents conduct fluency timings at home, they will acquire first-hand knowledge of their children's reading improvement on a daily basis.

Individual Fluency Programs

All struggling readers should have reading fluency practice as an instructional goal. However, the partnership model is not appropriate in all educational settings. In a special education, remedial, or resource room—where the students' instructional reading levels may be very diverse—it is often not possible to select evenly matched fluency partners. In these cases, individual fluency programs should be developed.

To establish an individual fluency program, the teacher will need to assess each student to determine the appropriate level for fluency practice. Students should be introduced to the concept of repeated reading and given a rationale as to why they will be engaging in the practice. Finally, each student will need his/her own fluency folder containing two *Practice Passages*—one for the student to read from and the other for the teacher to follow along with—a *Fluency Graph* (see *Appendix*), and a marking pen for filling in the graph each day.

There are two options for conducting individual fluency programs. With Option 1, all students read a *Practice Passage* at their own instructional level, and all students follow the same steps every day. With Option 2, all students read a *Practice Passage* at their own instructional level and then proceed through the steps at their own individual rate.

Option 1

- **Monday**—All students select a new *Practice Passage* at their own instructional level. Students read the passage on their own, underlining difficult or unknown words. The teacher meets with each student individually. The teacher reads the entire passage with the student for accuracy, modeling fluent reading. Then, the student reads the passage while being timed for one minute to obtain an initial cwpm score. The student graphs the cwpm number on his/her *Fluency Graph*.
- **Tuesday, Wednesday, and Thursday**—All students take turns reading their *Practice Passage* to the teacher while being timed for one minute. Each student then graphs the cwpm number on his/her *Fluency Graph*. When not meeting with the teacher, students practice whisper-reading their passage.
- **Friday**—All students take turns reading their *Practice Passage* to the teacher while being timed for one minute in order to obtain a final score. Each student then graphs the final cwpm number on that particular passage on his/her *Fluency Graph*.

Option 2

- **Step 1:** All students select a new *Practice Passage* at their own instructional level.
- **Step 2:** The teacher meets with each student individually and, together with each student, choral-reads the passage for accuracy (untimed).
- **Step 3:** Each student reads the passage to the teacher for one minute. The teacher tells the student how many cwpm he/she read. This is the student's initial score.
- **Step 4:** The teacher and the student select a target goal. The goal should be 20–40 words above the initial timing. For example, if a student reads 50 cwpm on an initial timing, the target goal could be 80. **Note:** Select a target goal that is reasonably attainable for the student, taking into consideration his/her reading level and motivation.
- **Step 5:** Every day during fluency practice, the student reads his/her *Practice Passage* to the teacher for one minute and graphs the cwpm on the *Fluency Graph*. When students reach their oral reading goal with fewer than three reading errors, they have passed the passage. **Note:** Some students may be able to fluently read a passage in one week or less, while others may need to practice reading the same passage for two or more consecutive weeks before they reach their predetermined goal.

CHAPTER 3

Introducing the Fluency Concept

This chapter provides a model for introducing the concept of fluency to students. Students deserve to be given an explanation prior to engaging in a new procedure. They are more likely to be enthusiastic participants when they understand the "what" and the "why." In the words of noted educator Dr. Anita Archer, "Rationale reduces resistance."

Materials:
- For kindergarten, beginning first-grade, and remedial students, use a *Letter/Sound Fluency Building Sheet* (see *Fluency Building Sheets*). For students in mid-first to third grade, use a *Practice Passage* (see *Fluency Building Sheets*).
- One copy of the selected *Letter/Sound Fluency Building Sheet* or *Practice Passage*, laminated or enclosed in a plastic sleeve, for each student in the class.
- An overhead transparency of the same *Letter/Sound Fluency Building Sheet* or *Practice Passage* and a transparency marker.
- One zipper-lock plastic bag for each student to store a dry-erase marker and a cloth square for erasing markings.
- A digital timer or stopwatch.
- An overhead transparency of "What Is Reading Fluency?" (see *Appendix*).
- An overhead transparency of "Why Is Reading Fluency Important?" (see *Appendix*).
- One copy of the *Fluency Graph* (see *Appendix*) for each student.
- An overhead transparency of the *Fluency Graph*.

Estimated Time:
20 + minutes.

Use Activity Procedure or Scripted Procedure

Activity Procedure:
1. **Select the *Letter/Sound Fluency Building Sheet* or *Practice Passage*.**
   Select one *Letter/Sound Fluency Building Sheet* or *Practice Passage* for classroom demonstration and training. For beginning readers, select a fluency sheet with randomly ordered letter names, letter sounds, or high-frequency words known by all students. If you are using a passage, the readability should match the lowest level of reading in the class. For example, in a second-grade class, if the student who reads at the lowest level reads at a beginning first-grade level, the passage selected for training should be a first-grade readability level. It is important that students do not struggle while reading the passage.
2. **Introduce the concept of fluency.**
   Using grade-appropriate vocabulary, introduce to students the value of building fluency. You may paraphrase the information provided in the *Introduction* section and discuss the benefits of rereading, the concept of "practice makes perfect," and the correlation of fluency, comprehension, and work completion.

Optional Scripted Procedure for Introducing the Concept of Fluency:

Show students the overhead transparency of "What Is Reading Fluency?" and say:

- "Our class will be starting a daily reading fluency program. Before I explain the program to you, I want to talk about what fluency is and why it is important. Reading fluency is the ability to read text accurately. That means that you know all of the words. Reading fluency is also the ability to read text quickly. However, fluency is not speed-reading. Good readers read quickly, but not too quickly. As readers, we want to be sure to stop at the punctuation marks and to read so that other people can understand what we are saying. That means that we need to clearly say each word, not read so fast that the words run together. We need to remember the three parts of fluent reading: reading accurately, quickly, and with expression."

- "Listen. When we read fluently, we are reading accurately, quickly, and with expression."

- "Everyone, when you read fluently, you are reading how?" (Students should respond, "accurately.") "You are also reading how?" (Students should respond, "quickly.") "But you are also reading with what, everyone?" (Students should respond, "with expression.")

- "So, reading fluently is reading accurately, quickly, and with expression."

- "Say it with me, everyone."

Show students the overhead transparency of "Why Is Reading Fluency Important?" and say:

- "It is important to work on improving reading fluency for three reasons. How many reasons?" (Students should respond, "three.") "The most important reason is because reading fluency is related to comprehension. Fluent readers understand what they are reading. Fluent readers have good what, everyone?" (Students should respond, "comprehension.") "If we can read the words easily or fluently, we can pay better attention to what we are reading. So the main reason that we are going to work on reading fluency is so we will improve our what, everyone? Our ... " (Students should respond, "comprehension.")

- "Fluent readers like to read because reading is easy for them. If reading is easy for us, we will read more and if we read more, we will learn more. So, another reason for improving reading fluency is to be able to read more independently. We are going to practice reading fluency so that we will become what kind of readers, everyone?" (Students should respond, "independent.")

- "Finally, fluent readers need less time to complete their class assignments and their homework. Fluent readers read faster, so they finish work faster and have more time for outside activities. Raise your hand if you would like to be able to finish your homework in less time. So, we will practice reading fluency so that we will improve our what?" (Students should respond, "work completion.")

3. **Explain the *Letter/Sound Fluency Building Sheet* or *Practice Passage*.**
   - Pass out copies of the selected *Letter/Sound Fluency Building Sheet* or *Practice Passage* to the class. Explain to students that the fluency sheet or passage has numbers at the beginning of each line in order to help them keep track of how many letter-sounds or words they read in one minute.
4. **Model the reading fluency procedure.**
   - Explain to students that when they read a *Letter/Sound Fluency Building Sheet* or *Practice Passage*, they will start with the first letter-sound on the fluency sheet or the first word of the passage and read until the timer sounds. As they read, they should track their reading with a pen (without making marks) and underline any unknown or difficult letter-sounds or words. When the timer sounds, they will draw a diagonal line after the last letter or word they read.
   - Demonstrate the above procedure on the overhead of the fluency sheet or passage.
   - Continue using the transparency to demonstrate **how to count the total number of letter-sounds or words read**. Starting at the number at the beginning of the last line read, simply count from that number to the last word or letter read. This is the total number of words or letters read. Count the number of underlined (i.e., difficult or incorrect) letter-sounds or words. Subtract the number of incorrect letter-sounds or words from the total number to determine the **correct number of letter-sounds or words read per minute**.

Optional Scripted Procedure for Presenting a Letter/Sound Fluency Building Sheet or Practice Passage:
   - "Listen. When we read a passage [fluency sheet], we will start with the first word [letter] (point) and read until the timer sounds. Where will we start, everyone?" (Students should respond, "the first word [letter].") "As we read, we should track with our finger or pen and be ready to underline any unknown or difficult words [letter-sounds]. A difficult word [letter-sound] is a word [letter-sound] that we cannot figure out within a couple of seconds. What will we do with difficult words [letter-sounds], everyone?" (Students should respond, "underline them.") "When the timer sounds, we will put a diagonal line after the last word [letter-sound] we read."
   - "Watch me." (Demonstrate on the overhead transparency of the fluency sheet or passage.)
   - "Next, we need to figure out the total number of correct words [letter-sounds] we read in one minute. To do this, we look at where we put the diagonal mark after the last word [letter-sound]. What do we do first, everyone?" (Students should respond, "find the last word [letter-sound] we read.") Then, we go back to the beginning of that line. Where do we go, everyone?" (Students should respond, "to the beginning of the last line we read.") "Now, we find the number count on that line. What do we find?" (Students should respond, "the number count on that line.") "Then, we count from that number to the last number read. That is the total number of words [letter-sounds]

we read. What is it?" (Students should respond, "the total number of words [letter-sounds] we read.") "We write that number of the line on the passage [fluency sheet]. Next, we count the number of underlined words [letter-sounds]. What do we count?" (Students should respond, "the number of underlined words [letter-sounds].") "Now, subtract the number of underlined words [letter-sounds] from the total number of words [letter-sounds] read. The answer gives us the number of correct words [letter-sounds] read per minute. What does it tell us?" (Students should respond, "the number of correct words [letter-sounds] read per minute.")

Total Words Read _____
– Underlined words_____
= CWPM

5. **Have students whisper-read the** *Letter-Sound Fluency Building Sheet* **or** *Practice Passage.*
   - Set the timer for one minute, and ask students to whisper-read the fluency sheet or passage by following the procedures of tracking, underlining unknown/difficult letter-sounds or words, and drawing a diagonal line after the last letter-sound or word read when the timer sounds. **Note:** Students must whisper-read in order to simulate oral reading.
   - Ask students to figure out the total number of letter-sounds or words read, subtract the number of underlined items, and determine the total correct number of letter-sounds or words read per minute. Monitor students carefully.
   - Set the timer again for one minute, and ask students to read the fluency sheet or passage again, beginning with the first letter or word.
   - When the timer sounds, ask students to determine their total correct letter-sounds or words read per minute.
   - Lead a group discussion about fluency practice. Ask students to raise their hands if their second score was higher. Solicit student reflection on why they might have read more letter-sounds or words per minute the second time.

Optional Scripted Procedure for Presenting Whisper-Reading:
   - "Now it is your turn. I am going to set the timer for one minute. When I tell you to begin, I want you to whisper-read the passage [fluency building sheet] beginning with the first word of the passage [the first letter or word of the fluency building sheet]. It is important that you whisper-read because we are practicing oral, not silent, reading. As you read, underline any unknown or difficult words [letters]. When the timer sounds, put a diagonal mark after the last word [letter-sound] you read. Let's check: Will you read silently?" (Students should respond, "no.") "How will you read?" (Students should respond, "whisper-read.") "What will you do when the timer sounds?" (Students should respond, "put a slash mark after the last word [letter-sound] read.")

- When the timer sounds, say," Put a diagonal mark after the last word [letter-sound] you read. Go back to the beginning of that line. Say the number and continue counting until you reach the last word [letter-sound] you read. That is your total number of words [letter-sounds]. Write that number down." Monitor students closely. "Now, go back to the beginning of the passage [fluency building sheet] and count the number of underlined words [letter-sounds]. Subtract that number from your total number of words [letter-sounds]." Monitor students closely. "Now you have your total number of correct words [letter-sounds] per minute. Write that number on the passage [fluency sheet]."

- "Now, you are going to whisper-read the passage again. Start at the same place with the first word [letter-sound], whisper-read, and underline unknown words [letter-sounds]. This time when the timer sounds, circle the last word [letter-sound] you read. Ready, please begin."

- When the timer sounds, say, "Circle the last word [letter-sound] you read. Go back to the beginning of that line. Say the number and continue counting until you reach the last word [letter-sound] read. That is your total number of words [letter-sounds]. Write that number down." Monitor students closely. "Now, go back to the beginning of the passage [fluency building sheet] and count the number of underlined words [letter-sounds]. Subtract that number from your total number of words [letter-sounds]." Monitor students closely. "Now you have your number of correct words [letter-sounds] per minute for your second reading. Write that number on the passage [fluency sheet]."

- "Compare your first timing score with your second timing score." Pause as students compare their scores. "Raise your hand if you read more words [letter-sounds] the second time than you read the first time." The vast majority of students will have read more the second time. "Turn to your neighbor (partner) and tell him/her why you think that you read more words [letter-sounds] the second time." Monitor students. "As I monitored, I heard many of you say that when you read the second time, you already knew the words [letter-sounds]. You were familiar with the passage so you could read faster the second time. There were no surprises on the second reading. You are exactly right. The more you practice a skill, the better you will become at that skill. So in order to become more fluent readers, we are going to practice every day."

6. **Demonstrate the graphing process.**
   - Distribute one copy of the *Fluency Graph* to each student.
   - Using the overhead transparency of the *Fluency Graph*, demonstrate how to record the number of correct letter-sounds or words read per minute.
   - Have students practice graphing their correct letter-sounds or words per minute on their first and second readings of the fluency sheet or passage. **Note:** Teachers of very young students may wish to use a simple record sheet instead of the *Fluency Graph*.

Optional Scripted Procedure for Presenting the Graphing Process:

- "Now, we are going to look at how to graph the number of correct words [letter-sounds] we read in one minute. Each one of you has a graph that looks like this (show the *Fluency Graph*). At the top, you will write your name, your partner's name, the class you are in, and the date you first started using this graph. For today's practice, just fill in your name."

- "Notice at the bottom of the graph, there is a place for the passage [fluency sheet] number and the date. Fill in the passage [fluency sheet] number and today's date. Since all of us read the same passage [fluency sheet] on the same day, we will have the same passage [fluency sheet] number and the same date."

- "Now, look at the numbers on the left side of the passage [fluency sheet]. Those are the number of correct words [letter-sounds] you read. What are the numbers for?" (Students should respond, "the correct number of words [letter-sounds] read.") "Now, look at the graph. Do you see a place for errors on this graph?" (Students should respond, "no.") "You will not be recording errors on the graph. You will subtract your errors from your total on the passage [fluency sheet] and record only the correct words [letter-sounds] per minute on the graph."

- "Do the numbers start with 1? (Students should respond, "no.") "What do they start with?" (Students should respond, "5.") "That's right, the numbers are in increments of 5. Let's pretend that I read 45 correct words per minute (cwpm) on my initial timing. Put your finger on the number 45. I will color in the squares from 5 to 45 to graph my initial timing. Now, let's pretend that on my second timing, I read 52 cwpm. Is the number 52 on the graph?" (Students should respond, "no.") "So I will have to estimate. To do that, I will go to the number closest to 52. What number will that be?" (Students should respond, "50.") "Then I will go just a little higher to show that I read more than 50 cwpm. This time, I will color in the squares from 5 to just past 50 to graph my second timing."

- "Now, it's your turn. Graph your first and second timing scores. Raise your hand if you need help." Walk around the room and monitor as students graph their numbers.

CHAPTER 4

Establishing Partner Behavior

In order for the partnership model to be successful, students need to work together in a polite and respectful manner. This chapter offers suggestions for introducing the concept of a working relationship within a cooperative partnership. Students need to be instructed in appropriate fluency partnership behavior (e.g., leaning in and whispering), remembering that the only people who need to hear them are their partners, and providing appropriate corrective feedback on missed words or letter-sounds. Addressing classroom noise level during training is key to preventing many potential problems. Teachers are often amazed at the low level of classroom noise when fluency timings are in progress.

Use Activity Procedure or Scripted Procedure

Activity Procedure:
1. Tell students that they will be working with a fluency partner for six minutes each day, emphasizing that the partnership is a working relationship and not necessarily a friendship. You may want to give an example of cooperation within a workplace, explaining that although we may not necessarily like everyone with whom we work and may not want to be close friends with, we still need to treat coworkers with respect. An explanation may be given that the partnerships were assigned based on assessment data and the fact that "the computer assigned the partners." **Note:** If the concept of fluency is discussed completely with the class, there are generally few problems within partnerships. However, very occasionally, there may be partners who simply do not work well together. In that case, partners may need to be reassigned.
2. Set rules about appropriate noise levels during fluency practice. Remind students that because half of the class will be reading aloud at the same time, the only people who will need to hear them are their fluency partners. Tell students that they will "lean in and whisper" when reading to their partners. Model the procedure, giving examples and non-examples.
3. Teach students to give polite feedback to each other by following this format: "You read ____ words [letter-sounds]. I heard ____ errors. Your score is ____ ."
4. Teach students this error-correction procedure: The partner points to the missed word [letter-sound] and says, "This word [letter-sound] is ____. What is the word [letter-sound]?"

Optional script for presenting expectations of fluency partnerships:
- "We are going to be working in partnerships to practice reading fluency for six minutes every day. Let me tell you about partnerships. Partnerships are two people working together. What are they, everyone?" (Students should respond, "two people working together.") "You do not have to be friends with your partners. You do not have to eat lunch together or walk down the hall together. You do not have to talk to each other outside of this class. But here is what you do need to do:

For the six minutes that you are working in the partnership, you have to be polite and respectful. What do you have to be?" (Students should respond, "polite and respectful.")

- "In your partnerships, one of you will be Partner 1 and one of you will be Partner 2. All Partners 1s will read at one time while all Partner 2s listen, follow along, and underline any errors. That means that half of the class will be reading at one time. If all Partner 1s read in a regular speaking voice, is it possible that the noise level in the room will be too high? Yes or no?" (Students should respond, "yes.") "In order to keep the level down so that partners can hear each other read, you will lean in and whisper. What will you do?" (Students should respond, "lean in and whisper.")

- Choose a student partner to demonstrate the procedure. "I am (Juan's) partner. Watch me read to Juan." Demonstrate reading in a regular voice while looking straight ahead. "Did I lean in and whisper? Yes or no?" (Students should respond, "no.") "Watch me again." Demonstrate the correct procedure. "Did I lean in and whisper?" (Students should respond, "yes.")

- "While your partner is reading, you will follow along and underline any errors you hear. What will you do?" (Students should respond, "follow along and underline errors.") "When the timer sounds, you will draw a diagonal line after the last word or letter-sound your partner reads. What will you do when the timer sounds?" (Students should respond, "draw a diagonal line after the last word or letter-sound my partner reads.") "Then you will figure out your partner's correct words or letter-sounds per minute. What will you do?" (Students should respond, "figure out the correct words or letter-sounds per minute.")

- "The next step is reporting to your partner. What is the next step?" (Students should respond, "reporting to your partner.")

- "First, you will tell your partner the total number of words or letter-sounds that he/she read. Say, 'You read ____ words [letter-sounds].' What do you say?" (Students repeat.) "Then you say, 'I heard ____ errors.' What do you say?" (Students repeat.) "Why do you suppose I want you to say 'I heard ____ errors' rather than 'You made ____ errors'?" (Students should suggest that it sounds better.) "Yes, it sounds kinder. Then you tell your partner their correct words or letter-sounds per minute. That is the number they will graph at the end of the reading session."

- "Finally, you will point to any reading errors your partner made, one word at a time, and pronounce the words correctly for your partner. Your partner will then read the words again correctly."

- "There is one very important rule that you need to know when working with your partner. The rule is: **No arguing**. What is the rule?" (The students should respond, "no arguing.") "The reason why we have a 'No arguing' rule is that arguing wastes time. What does it do?" (Students should respond, "it wastes time."). "If my partner underlines a word or letter-sound that I think I read correctly, I could stop reading and tell my partner that he or she made a mistake. But if I do that, I will miss the rest of my timing for that day and I won't be able to record a score.

So, if I think that my partner hears a word or letter-sound incorrectly, it is counted as an error because there is no what?" (Students should respond, "no arguing."). "The best thing for partners to do is to treat each other fairly."

- Taking the time to properly train students in *Six-Minute Solution Primary* procedures will ensure that the program runs smoothly. It is important that students be taught the correct fluency procedures. Once students are properly trained, the entire fluency practice should take only six minutes of the reading period each day.

CHAPTER 5

Training Students in the Partnership Model

Taking the time to properly train students in *Six-Minute Solution Primary* partnership procedures will ensure a smoothly running program. Once students are trained, the entire fluency practice should take only six minutes of the reading period each day. This chapter discusses how to teach fluency procedures to students.

Devote a *minimum* of two or three class periods to student training. It is recommended that an explicit instructional model be employed. The procedures should be introduced through modeling followed by considerable guided practice time, with the teacher monitoring student participation, giving feedback, and remodeling as necessary so that students can practice the procedures independently.

Materials:
- Two laminated copies of a *Practice Passage* at the readability level of the lowest reader in the class;
  OR
  Two laminated copies of a fluency building sheet with randomly ordered letters/sounds (*Letter/Sound Fluency Building Sheets*), phonetic elements (*Phonetic Elements Fluency Building Sheets*), or automatic words (*Automatic Words Fluency Building Sheets*) known by all students. (All fluency building sheets can be found in *Fluency Building Sheets*.)
- A copy of a *Phonetic Elements Record Graph*, *Automatic Words Record Graph*, *Fluency Record*, or *Fluency Graph* for each student partner. (All of these items can be found in the *Appendix*.) **Note:** If students are being trained to use *Practice Passages*, use a *Fluency Record* or a *Fluency Graph*. If students are practicing phonetic elements, use a *Phonetic Elements Record Graph*. If students are practicing automatic words, use an *Automatic Words Record Graph*.
- A zipper-lock plastic bag containing a dry-erase marking pen and a small piece of cloth for erasing marks or a small piece of dampened sponge and a washable ink pen for each student pair.
- An overhead transparency of the selected reading passage or fluency building sheet.
- An overhead transparency of the scoring record or graph and a dry-erase marker.
- A digital timer or stopwatch.

Use Activity Procedure or Scripted Procedure

Activity Procedure:
1. Seat each student with a fluency partner—random or selected—and label the partners as Partner 1 and Partner 2.
2. Model the fluency partnership with a student partner, emphasizing how the listener should accurately track the words/letters/sounds the partner reads. Tracking helps students keep their place as they silently read along with the reading partner and makes marking errors easier.

3. Review with students:
- The procedure for marking errors and noting the stopping point.
- The process of word counting and error reporting (see *Figure 5.1*).
- How to calculate the correct words/letters/sounds per minute (cwpm) by determining the total number of words/letters/sounds read and then subtracting errors. For example:

Total Words Read	*35*
– Errors	*2*
= CWPM	*33*

- How to use the scoring record or graph.

Figure 5.1
AN EXAMPLE OF THE ERROR-CORRECTION PROCEDURE

While the reader is reading aloud for one minute, the fluency partner follows along and underlines any errors. When the timer sounds, the partner notes the last word read, then provides feedback in the following manner.

Partner: "You read _____ (total number of) words. You made _____ (number of) errors." The partner then points to each underlined (incorrect) word and pronounces it correctly for the reader.

Reader: Records the cwpm on the *Fluency Graph*.

Note: Establish a "No arguing" rule between partners at this point in the training.

---

4. Practice with students:
- Set the timer for one minute, and ask all Partner 1s to read. Remind them to lean in toward their partner and whisper-read. Remind Partner 2s to track their partner's reading accuracy.
- Instruct Partner 2s to give polite feedback to Partner 1s.
- Set the timer again for one minute, and instruct Partner 2s to read. Remind them to lean in toward their partner and whisper-read. Remind Partner 1s to track their partner's reading accuracy.
- Instruct Partner 1s to give polite feedback to Partner 2s.

Optional Scripted Procedure for training students:
1. Select a student partner with whom to read, and instruct her/him to make a few reading errors. Say:
- "Watch as my partner Sarita and I conduct our fluency timings. Sarita is Partner 1, so she will read first. Watch what I do while she is reading."
2. Set the timer for one minute, and ask the student partner to begin reading.
3. Model the tracking of the partner's reading with the marking pen, underlining the reading errors as the student partner reads and drawing a diagonal line at the partner's stopping point when the timer sounds.

4. After the timer sounds, say:
   - " What did you observe me doing with my pen as my partner was reading?" (Students should respond, "tracking.")
   - "Yes, it is important to follow along by tracking under each word as my partner reads. What did I do when I heard an error?" (Students should respond, "you underlined it.")
   - "Yes, I underlined the error and kept tracking. Did I make any extra marks on the sheet?" (Students should respond, "no.")
   - "I made a mark only if I heard an error. If I had drawn a line under each word my partner read, would I have been able to tell when she made an error? Yes or no?" (Students should respond, "no."). "Also, marking under all the words would be messy and hard to clean off in only one minute."
   - "Listen to me give polite feedback to Sarita: You read 76 words. I heard two errors. 76 − 2 = 74. 74 is your score. Mark that on your graph. You will color in the squares later."
   - "Now I need to tell Sarita the words she missed and ask her to repeat them." Point to the first error and say, "This word is ____ . What word?"
   - "Now it is your turn. Raise your hand if you are a Partner 1. Raise your hand if you are a Partner 2. When I say 'Please begin,' all Partner 1s will lean in and whisper-read to their partners. All Partner 2s should have their pen and be ready to follow along, marking your partner's errors and the stopping point. Please begin."
5. After the timer sounds, say:
   - "All Partner 2s give polite feedback to Partner 1s." (Partner 2s give Partner 1s their scores. Partner 1s mark their graphs. Monitor the conversational exchanges.)
   - "Now it is Partner 2s turn. When I say 'Please begin,' all Partner 2s lean in and whisper-read to their partners. All Partner 1s should have the pen and be ready to follow along, marking your partner's errors and the stopping point. Please begin."
6. After the timer sounds, say:
   - "Now Partner 1s should give polite feedback to Partner 2s." (Partner 1s give Partner 2s their scores. Partner 2s mark their graphs. Monitor the conversational exchanges.)
7. One partner from each partnership puts away all materials.

Note: Continue these practice sessions with students until they are comfortable with their partner roles, determining number counts, and recording scores. Remember that the goal is for students to be able to complete the procedure in only six minutes.

CHAPTER 6

Managing Materials

Well-organized materials that are easily accessible to the primary student will assist in the establishment of effective fluency routines. Ideas for initial implementation and ongoing management of *Six-Minute Solution Primary* materials are included in this chapter.

Teacher Preparation

- Set up files for fluency sheets and reading passages. Determine which level of fluency sheets and reading passages are needed for the class, then make multiple copies of them and file them. Organize your files by readability or phonetic element. Color-coding is a very effective visual aid when setting up detailed filing systems.
- Make one portfolio—a folder with pockets—for each student partnership. Each portfolio should hold two copies of the same fluency sheet or reading passage; two copies of the *Fluency Record, Fluency Graph*, or *Partner Points Sheet* (depending on which of the three is to be used; all are found in the *Appendix*); and a zipper-lock plastic bag containing a dry-erase marker and a small piece of cloth.
- Set up a file for reading passages organized by readability level.
- Set up a central location to store the portfolios.

Teacher Demonstration

- Show the class where the partnership portfolios will be kept.
- Demonstrate the procedure for turning in old fluency sheets or reading passages on Fridays: (1) one partner takes the old fluency sheets or reading passages out of the enclosed plastic sleeves and, also in the case of old laminated fluency sheets or reading passages, returns them to a designated file; (2) the other partner selects two copies of a different fluency sheet or reading passage of the same level to be used the next week. **Note:** Only one of the partners should perform both tasks. If not, there will be too many students at the filing location at the same time.

Additional Fluency Tips

- Once students are trained in the *Six-Minute Solution Primary* Instructional Format (see *Table I.1* in the *Introduction* section), use the *Six-Minute Solution Primary* Sample Schedule (also in the *Introduction*). It is most effective and efficient for students to begin reading a *Fluency Building Sheet, Assessment Passage*, or *Practice Passage* on the first day of the school week.
- Make certain that each partnership knows who is Partner 1 and who is Partner 2. Partner 1 is the stronger reader and always reads first. Do not share that information with students, however; simply state that Partner 1 reads first for management purposes.
- Tell students where they will sit during fluency practice. For example, some teachers make a seating arrangement for the language arts period that places partners next to each other. Other teachers have Partner 1s move next to Partner 2s' desks.

- Begin the first fluency practice session of the week with an accuracy check. Have students read the fluency sheet or reading passage (untimed) to determine any unknown or difficult words. If neither one of the partners knows a word, supply it for them. This accuracy check should occur only on the first day of a new fluency sheet or reading passage each week.

- Remember that students need a minimum of three to five repeat readings of the same fluency sheet or reading passage. Since both student partners will have the same fluency sheet or reading passage, both will hear it read twice each day. Fluency sheets or passages should be changed once a week so that students are not able to memorize the material. **Note:** The reading level of the *Practice Passage* is changed only after teacher review and assessment.

- Remind students that they are responsible for keeping to the six-minute time frame:
  - One minute for the partners to get ready.
  - One minute for Partner 1 to read.
  - One minute for Partner 2 to tell Partner 1 the total number of words read, the errors, corrections, and cwpm. Partner 1 quickly records his/her cwpm.
  - One minute for Partner 2 to read.
  - One minute for Partner 1 to tell Partner 2 the total number of words read, the errors, corrections, and cwpm. Partner 2 quickly records his/her cwpm.
  - One minute for both partners to color in their own graphs and put materials away.

- Generally speaking, fluency partners provide accountability for each other. Occasionally, a partnership may appear to be awarding inflated scores. A word or two in private to the "suspects" should solve the problem along with maintaining close proximity while the partnership is conducting its timings.

- *Continually* monitor students closely during the six-minute fluency practices.

CHAPTER 7

Student Progress and Record Keeping

Record keeping is an essential component of the *Six-Minute Solution Primary*. It is critical to monitor improvement and make instructional decisions based on individual student progress. This may be accomplished by using either the *Fluency Record* or the *Fluency Graph* (see the *Appendix*). Teach students how to graph their own progress. Students tend to enjoy using the *Fluency Records* and *Fluency Graphs,* as they make it easy for them to see their progress. Graphs can be especially motivating to students who have not had much reading success in the past. It gives them a concrete way to see their reading skills improve.

As a general rule, students who repeatedly read *Phonetic Elements/ Automatic Words Fluency Building Sheets* or *Practice Passages* at the correct instructional level make weekly progress—even if only by an increase of a few correct words per minute. Give special attention to any student whose reading rates are not increasing from week to week.

Determine whether students are reading at the expected rate for their instructional reading levels (see *Table 1.1* in *Chapter 1*). Remember, students should read at the rate commensurate with their *instructional reading levels*, not their grade-level placements. Reading rates increase as students are able to read more difficult material.

Check your students' *Fluency Records* or *Fluency Graphs* on a regular basis in order to determine that:

- Adequate progress is being made.
- Students have been assigned appropriate *Phonetic Elements/Automatic Words Fluency Building Sheets* or *Practice Passages*—neither too easy nor too difficult.
- Students have been assigned appropriate fluency partners.
- It is the appropriate time to increase the difficulty level of the *Phonetic Elements/Automatic Words Fluency Building Sheets* or *Grade-Level Practice Passages* being used by partners.

Making Instructional Decisions Based on Fluency Graphs

The following examples demonstrate how the information on a student's *Fluency Record* or *Fluency Graph* can help you make important instructional decisions.

Example 1: David

David is a second-grade student with a first-grade instructional reading level. Based on *Table 1.1* (Hasbrouck & Tindal, 2005) in *Chapter 1*, he is within the expected reading rate for his instructional level. David is also making adequate progress (see *Figure 7.1*). The first five days on his *Fluency Graph* reflect rereading the same *Practice Passage*. His first reading on Monday was 60 cwpm. After practicing the passage four more times, his ending fluency rate was 70 cwpm.

Notice what happened the following week (see March 9 column), when David began reading a new first-grade *Practice Passage*. His beginning fluency rate has increased by five words (from 60 to 65 cwpm) when compared to the previous Monday—even though this is a new passage. As he continued to reread this passage during the second week, David's reading rate steadily improved. As David's reading rate continues to improve and he begins to approach and pass 75 cwpm on his weekly passages, he will most likely be ready to start practicing second-grade *Practice Passages*.

Figure 7.1
David's Fluency Graph
Practice Passage: Level 1

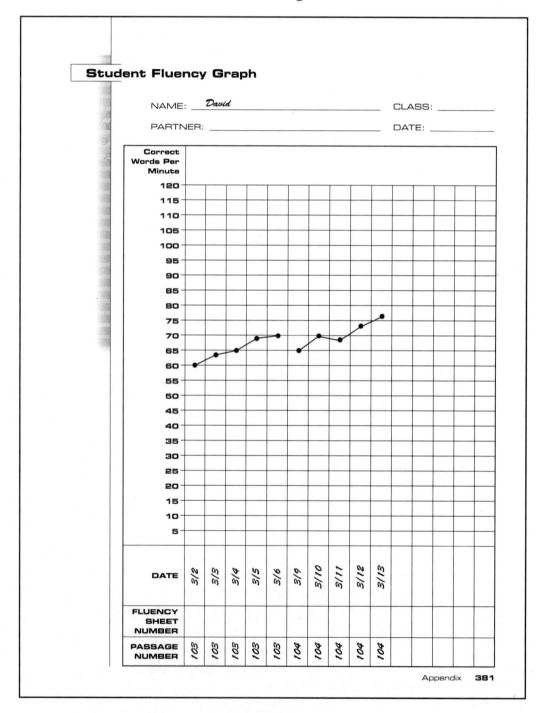

Example 2: Sarita

Sarita is reading at a third-grade instructional reading level and was assigned a third-grade *Practice Passage. Based* on *Table 1.1* (Hasbrouck & Tindal, 2005) in *Chapter 1*, the appropriate goal for Sarita to read third-grade material in the spring of the school year is at least 107 cwpm.

A glance at Sarita's *Fluency Graph* (*Figure 7.2*) reveals that she is reading significantly below her expected range. In this case, the teacher decides that he needs to reevaluate whether or not Sarita has been placed correctly at her instructional level. Based on this reevaluation, the teacher will decide whether or not to: (1) lower the *Practice Passage* reading level; (2) add practice with *Automatic Words Fluency Building Sheets*; or (3) incorporate additional instructional strategies such as the ones in the following section, "Helping the Student Who Is Not Making Adequate Progress."

Figure 7.2
Sarita's Fluency Graph
Practice Passage: 305

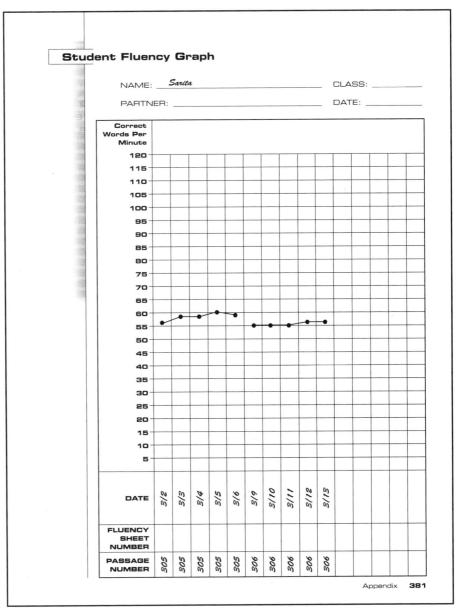

Example 3: José

José is a first-grade student with a first-grade instructional reading level. His minimum fluency goal in the spring of the school year as shown in *Table 1.1* (Hasbrouck & Tindal, 2005) in *Chapter 1* is 53 cwpm. When José's teacher reviewed his *Fluency Graph* (*Figure 7.3*), she noticed that his reading rate was above his goal rate. She decided to assign second-grade instructional reading level *Practice Passages* to José, which may be more challenging for him.

Figure 7.3
José's Fluency Graph
Practice Passage: Level 1

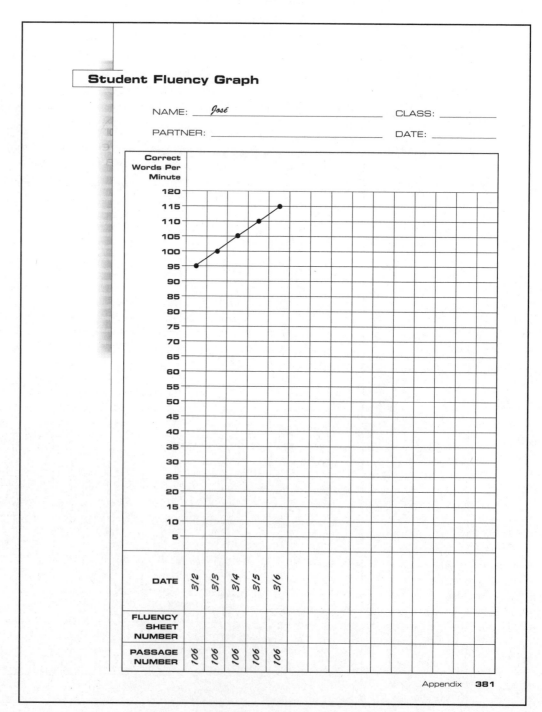

Helping the Student Who Is Not Making Adequate Progress

If a student is not making progress in the *Six-Minute Solution Primary* word building or passage fluency activities, it may be that the assigned *Fluency Building Sheets* or *Practice Passages* do not match the student's *instructional reading level*. Students must be placed at the correct instructional reading levels in order to make the expected progress. When students practice fluency at their correct instructional levels, the vast majority makes excellent progress. However, if after examining a student's *Fluency Graph* or *Fluency Record* you determine that little progress has been made in two or more weeks, consider the following:

- Ensure that the student is receiving comprehensive reading instruction in addition to the *Six-Minute Solution Primary*.
- Read the *Fluency Building Sheet* or *Practice Passage* with the student to ascertain if he/she has been placed at the correct instructional reading level. The student should be able to correctly read approximately 95% of the words at the appropriate instructional level. Note the errors the student is making. Perhaps many of the words the student is having difficulty with are high-frequency sight words. In this case, the student is likely to benefit from additional practice with *Automatic Words Fluency Building Sheets*. These lists contain sets of the most commonly encountered (i.e., high-frequency) words in the written English language.
- If you observe that a student is having great difficulty reading an assigned *Fluency Building Sheet* or *Practice Passage*, have the student practice with a fluency sheet or passage that is one grade level below the current one. If the student reads less than 95% of the words correctly in the new fluency sheet or passage, have him/her read one at an even lower reading level.
- A student's reading fluency problems may be associated with poor decoding skills. Assess whether the student would benefit from extra instruction in decoding or in using *Phonetic Elements Fluency Building Sheets*.
- When students are first presented with a new *Fluency Building Sheet* or *Practice Passage*, make a point of meeting with the partnerships of struggling readers to ensure that they are demonstrating adequate accuracy. Consistently and carefully monitor partnerships of struggling readers throughout the week.
- A stronger reader may be paired with a struggling reader as a practice partner. The stronger reader reads the *Fluency Building Sheet* or *Practice Passage* while the struggling reader follows closely behind, echoing the words of the stronger reader. The struggling reader gains additional reading strength by having the fluency sheet or passage read almost simultaneously. The practice partnership session would occur in addition to the regular *Six-Minute Solution Primary* session.
- Give fluency partners extra untimed reading-practice opportunities. Partners can whisper-read to each other, thus gaining additional rereadings of the same *Fluency Building Sheet* or *Practice Passage* before taking their formal one-minute timings. Additional practice sessions help to build the confidence of struggling readers.

- Fluency partners may also "ping-pong read" sentences back and forth to each other as another form of practice. This also helps them gain confidence and familiarity with the *Fluency Building Sheet* or *Practice Passage* prior to the formal fluency timing.

CHAPTER 8

Comprehension and Writing Strategies

Comprehension strategies (e.g., summarizing and paraphrasing) and the use of graphic organizers can be taught and practiced using the *Practice Passages* in the *Six-Minute Solution Primary*. It is recommended that students be taught comprehension strategies and how to use graphic organizers directly through modeling and guided practice, and then bolstered by independent practice. Examples of effective comprehension strategies for nonfiction include:

- Summarizing
- Paraphrasing
- Retelling
- Describing
- Learning expository text structure

Summarizing

One method to improve students' comprehension skills is to teach *summarizing*. First, model summarizing by pausing after reading aloud each paragraph of a *Practice Passage* from an overhead transparency. Then "think aloud" while you determine the main idea of each paragraph. It is important to limit the number of words in the summary. Counting the words as they are spoken is a powerful way to illustrate this concept. Another effective way of teaching summarizing is the use of "paragraph-shrinking" (Fuchs, Fuchs, Kazlan, & Allen, 1999).

Once you have modeled summarizing, you can assign each partner an alternate paragraph to summarize from their *Practice Passage*. Then, have the partners practice summarizing the whole passage. Encourage them to formulate a summary statement about the entire passage.

With additional instruction, this oral summarization practice can be extended to summary writing. After students complete their oral summarizations, ask them to turn over the *Practice Passage* and write a short summary of it.

Paraphrasing

To model *paraphrasing*, read aloud a *Practice Passage*—paragraph by paragraph—from an overhead transparency. After reading each paragraph, stop and announce, "I can put the information from this paragraph into my own words by saying … ."

Point out to students that it is easier to learn new information when you put it into your own words instead of trying to remember the text's language. Now have partners paraphrase alternate paragraphs of their *Practice Passages*.

Another effective method for teaching paraphrasing is to use the "read-cover-write-check" strategy for the *Skills for School Success Series* (Archer & Gleason, 2002).

Retelling

Read aloud a *Practice Passage* from an overhead transparency. Then, model a brief *retelling* of the passage, using the main ideas of each paragraph to formulate the retelling. By using phrases such as "The passage begins with … ,"

"Next, I read … ," and "Then I learned … ," you can effectively model retelling of information.

Describing

You can model *describing* by listing the characteristics, features, and examples of a topic. As you model, include key vocabulary words and phrases generally found in descriptive texts, such as "for example," "characteristics," "for instance," "such as," and "to illustrate." You may use a spider-web graphic organizer (as in *Figure 8.1*) in which the topic of the passage is listed in a circle in the center and the features are written on lines extending out from the circle, forming a "web."

Figure 8.1
Spider-Web Graphic Organizer

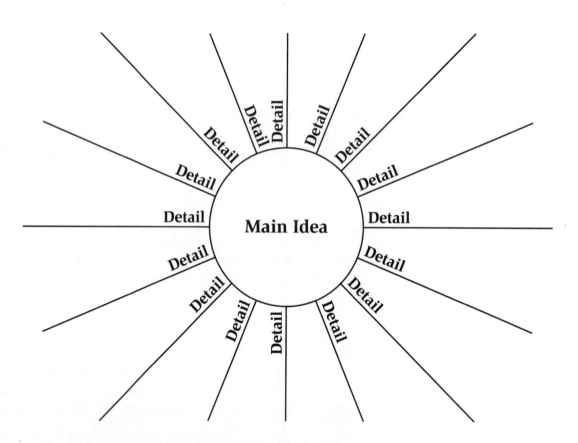

Students can take turns orally describing their *Practice Passage* paragraphs to their partners while the partners take notes on the passage.

Learning Expository Text Structure

Students can be taught about how text is structured using the following methods:

- Sequencing
- Comparing
- Analyzing cause and effect
- Problem-solving

Sequencing

Some of the *Practice Passages* list items or events in numerical or chronological order. When teaching students a comprehension strategy for this type of passage, call attention to key vocabulary words such as "first," "second," "third," "next," "then," "finally," "yesterday," "today," "now," "later," "before," and "after." Extend this sequencing comprehension activity to include writing by using a graphic organizer to list information sequentially (see *Figure 8.2*).

Figure 8.2
Sequencing Graphic Organizer

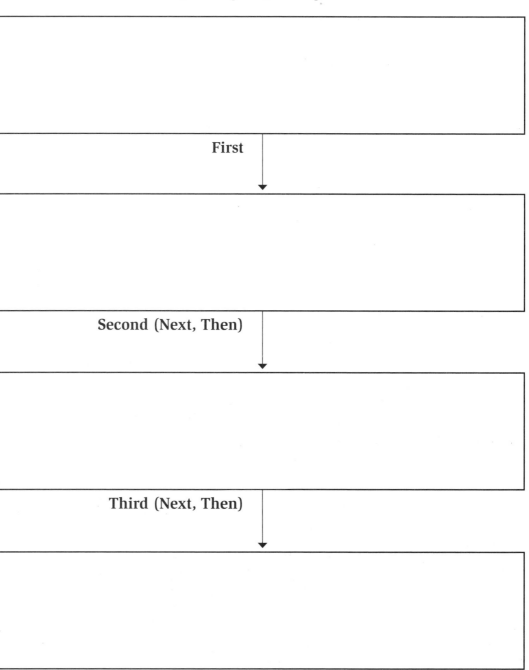

First

Second (Next, Then)

Third (Next, Then)

Fourth (Finally)

Comparing

Some of the *Practice Passages* explain how two or more things are alike or different. Call attention to key vocabulary in these passages such as "alike," "same as," "different from," "in contrast," "on the other hand," "but," "yet," "however," "although," "opposite of," "as well as," "while," and "unless." Venn diagrams are excellent graphic organizers to use for showing the similarities and differences in comparison text. A Venn diagram consists of two or more overlapping circles (see *Figure 8.3*).

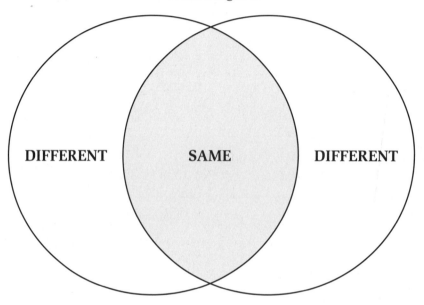

Figure 8.3
Venn Diagram

Analyzing Cause and Effect

Another type of expository text structure lists one or more causes and the resulting effect(s). Key vocabulary for this type of text includes "consequently," "because," "if ... then," "thus," "since," "nevertheless," "accordingly," "because of," "as a result of," "may be due to," "therefore," and "this led to." A graphic organizer may be used to illustrate cause and effect (see *Figure 8.4*).

Figure 8.4
Cause and Effect Graphic Organizer

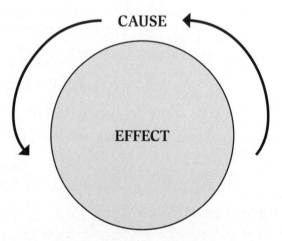

Problem-Solving

This type of expository text structure states a problem and lists one or more solutions. Key vocabulary includes "the problem is," " the question is," "furthermore," "one reason for," "a solution," and "another possibility." An example of a graphic organizer for a problem-solution text is shown in *Figure 8.5*.

Figure 8.5
Problem-Solving Graphic Organizer

Problem:

Solutions:

Summary Writing Strategies

Teachers may elect to incorporate summary-writing strategies into the *Six-Minute Solution Primary* fluency model. In that case, on the last day of fluency practice, partners write a short summary of the assigned *Practice Passage*. It is recommended that teachers demonstrate summary writing with a *Practice Passage* whose readability matches the reading level of the lowest reader in the class.

Activity procedure:

- Each student has a copy of the demonstration passage and a copy of the Summary Paragraph Frame (following).
- The teacher introduces the Summary Paragraph Frame and discusses each part.
- Students and teacher read the demonstration passage together.
- The teacher models filling in the Sample Paragraph Frame by thinking aloud.
- Students follow along and fill in their Summary Paragraph Frame.
- The teacher and students write a summary paragraph based on the Summary Paragraph Frame.

Summary Paragraph Frame 1

This passage was about _____. First, I learned _____. Next, I learned _____ . Finally, I learned _____.

Summary Paragraph Frame 2

Topic sentence (name the "who" or the "what"). Tell the most important thing about the "who" or the "what."

Example:

Reading is a very useful skill. One important fact is _____.

Another important fact is _____. A final important fact is _____.

CHAPTER 9

Building Letter/Sound Fluency

The first steps a student takes down the path to literacy begin with building an automatic knowledge of letters and the sounds they represent. It is not enough that a student can reproduce the letter symbols and their related sounds; a student must also do so quickly, automatically, and accurately—every time.

This chapter of the *Six-Minute Solution Primary* is divided into two parts. The first part contains specific directions for introducing letters/sounds to students who do not know them. The second part contains directions for using the *Letter/Sound Fluency Building Sheets* (see *Fluency Building Sheets*) to help those same students identify letters and sounds quickly, automatically, and accurately.

Introduction of Unknown Letters/Sounds

Materials:
- Various forms of targeted letters (e.g., magnetic letters, felt letters, letter cards)
- Word lists found at the end of this chapter
- White boards
- Dry-erase markers

Lesson Format

Step 1: Presentation of a New Letter/Sound
- Begin the lesson by modeling the new letter/sound. Hold up a letter card or write the letter on a white board. Say:
  - "This letter is 'm' and it says /m/. What is this letter?" (Students respond, "m.")
  - "What does it say?" (Students respond, "/m/.")
  - "Say its name with me." (Students respond, "m.")
  - "Say its sound with me." (Students respond, "/m/.")
- Repeat this modeling and practice together multiple times. Keep it quick and to the point.

Step 2: Group Practice of the New Letter/Sound
- Elicit individual and group responses for more practice. For example:
  - "Everyone who's wearing something blue, say this letter's name."
  - "Write the letter that says '/m/'."
  - "When I touch this letter on the board, say its sound."
- Use letters made up of different materials such as magnetic letters and felt letters.
- Check for accuracy by pronouncing words and asking students for a thumbs-up or thumbs-down response if the word does or does not begin with the letter/sound of choice.
- Have students continue to practice the new letter/sound for the next few days until they know it automatically.

Step 3: Independent Practice of the New Letter/Sound
- Reinforce the new letter and sound daily with a quick, focused practice session. For example:

– "Show me the letter that says '/m/,' and write the letter that says '/m/' three times on your white boards."

Step 4: Review of Letters/Sounds

- Incorporate previously taught letters and sounds—along with a new letter/sound—into a daily quick, focused practice session. Pronouncing words and asking students to hold up or write the correct beginning letters/sounds will enhance their letter knowledge.

Using the Letter/Sound Fluency Building Sheets

The *Letter/Sound Fluency Building Sheets* have been organized to enable students to practice letter names and/or letter sounds. Depending on the student's grade level, you may elect to have the student simply identify the sheet's letters by name, repeating them as quickly and accurately as possible. The individual letter sounds could be practiced in the same manner. The sheets can also be used to have students identify both the letter names and the letter sounds at the same time. Here are some suggestions for using the *Letter/Sound Fluency Building Sheets*:

- Introduce the letter names or letter sounds (or both) on a particular fluency sheet with direct instruction.
- Model the first two lines and then have students repeat them.
- Model the letter names and/or sounds and have students repeat them in an "echo" fashion.
- Instruct students to whisper-read the fluency sheet, marking the last letter/sound read when a timer sounds. Have students record their scores on a *Phonetic Elements Record Graph* (see *Appendix*), which they should store in a folder.
- Instruct students to whisper-read each row of the fluency sheet until they can *accurately* read the entire sheet in one minute or less.
- Train a student peer to be a "checker." The checker's job is to listen to a student read the fluency sheet and give an OK when the student can read it correctly in one minute or less. The student must "check out" with the teacher before moving on to the next fluency sheet. (The teacher listens to the student read the fluency sheet to determine if the student is 100% accurate in one minute or less.)

Partner Practice:

- Assign partners based on assessment results.
- Train partners in the *Six-Minute Solution Primary* fluency concept (see *Chapter 3*).
- Provide time each day for partner practice with the *Letter/Sound Fluency Building Sheets*. Have student partners practice reading their assigned fluency sheets to each other, correct each other's errors, and record their own number of letters/sounds read correctly in one minute on a *Phonetic Elements Record Graph*. Have students store the graph in a folder.

Small-Group Practice:

- Assign students to practice groups based on their assessment results.
- Introduce the letter names/sounds on the fluency sheet and have each group quietly "echo" each letter name, letter sound, or both. Student groups can then chant the entire fluency sheet together, moving to the next letter at the sound of a tap made by the teacher.

- Form partnerships within each small group by having students take turns practicing the fluency sheet with the student sitting next to him/ her. Time the students as they read to their partners, and then have them record their times on the *Phonetic Elements Record Graph* in their folders.
- Number the students within each group, and direct the number 1 students to read the first line, the number 2 students to read the second line, and so on, down the sheet for additional fluency practice.
- Divide each group, and direct the first half to read the first six lines of a fluency sheet and the second half to read the last six lines.
- Organize the small groups in a variety of ways (e.g., boys only, girls only, alphabetically by name, wearing the color yellow today) so that students have fun practicing the letter names/sounds.

Other Instructional Activities/Suggestions for Using the *Letter/Sound Fluency Building Sheets*

- Using pictures cut out of old magazines, have students make an "Alphabet Book." Students write a letter at the top of a sheet of paper and paste magazine pictures of objects whose spellings contain that letter/ sound. (This is also an excellent homework activity.) Letters/sounds that students have already mastered can simply be skipped in the Alphabet Book.
- Time students individually to ensure that they have the letters/sounds down to an automatic level. The goal should be to correctly pronounce 60 letter names/sounds they are practicing within one minute. Record student scores on the *Phonetic Elements Record Graph* in their folders.
- Introduce hands-on instructional activities to help students gain letter/ sound knowledge. For example, have students sort magnetic letters into different types of categories: all short letters, all tall letters, all consonant letters, all vowel letters, all uppercase letters, all lowercase letters, in alphabet sequence, etc.
- Enlist parent volunteers, older students, aides, or more proficient classmates to work with individual students, partnerships, or small groups.
- Send the *Letter/Sound Fluency Building Sheets* home for parents to help their children build letter/sound recognition to an automatic level. **Note:** It is important that students go home knowing how to correctly pronounce the letters/sounds. The sole purpose of the "homework" is to build recognition fluency of the letters/sounds.
- Use the following word lists when presenting letters and sounds.

Beginning Sounds Word Lists

Aa	Bb	Cc	Dd	Ee
ant	bat	cow	duck	elf
add	balloon	cap	dog	elk
apple	bank	cat	dust	elm
as	basket	cave	dock	end
at	beach	castle	dime	Ed
and	beads	cartoon	deer	enchant
ash	broom	car	dollar	exit

Ff	Gg	Hh	Ii	Jj
fog	gate	hat	if	jump
fish	goose	hair	is	jacket
feather	guitar	hammer	infect	jeep
five	gold	hay	in	joke
fire	gas	head	it	jail
football	goal	hall	imp	jam
fan	goat	ham	ill	job

Kk	Ll	Mm	Nn	Oo
kite	ladder	mop	nickel	on
kangaroo	lamp	mail	nap	ox
kettle	lemon	marble	name	odd
king	lake	map	needle	oxygen
kitten	log	milk	noise	otter
key	lunch	mirror	nose	often
kit	leaf	moon	nurse	octopus

Pp	Qq	Rr	Ss	Tt
pig	quick	rock	sun	table
paint	queen	rabbit	sack	top
peach	quiz	ranch	seed	tomato
pillow	quack	rat	seven	telephone
pickle	quaint	robe	sink	toe
pencil	quake	rocket	soup	tail
pipe	quiet	race	seal	tape

Uu	Vv	Ww	Xx	Yy
up	vase	wagon	box	yam
us	van	wall	sax	yawn
umpire	valentine	web	six	yellow
ugly	vine	week	xylophone	yard
umbrella	vote	wife	wax	yo-yo
upon	voice	wire	mix	year
under	violin	window	fox	yarn

Zz
zebra
zinc
zoom
zipper
zoo
zero
zip

CHAPTER 10

Building Phonetic Elements Fluency

The *Phonetic Elements Fluency Building Sheets* (see *Fluency Building Sheets*) in this program provide a quick and easy format to enable students to practice phonetic elements. This chapter is divided into two parts. The first part contains specific directions for introducing phonetic elements to students. The second part contains directions for using the *Phonetic Elements Fluency Building Sheets* to help students identify phonetic elements quickly, automatically, and accurately.

Introduction of Unknown Phonetic Elements

Materials:
- Various forms of the phonetic element being taught (e.g., magnetic letters, flash cards, phonetic elements cards, felt letters)
- White boards
- Dry-erase markers

Lesson Format
Step 1: Presentation of a New Phonetic Element
- Begin the lesson by modeling and teaching the new phonetic element or pattern. Hold up a card with the element on it, or write the element on a white board. Say:
  - "This letter [letters, pattern] says _____. What letters make up this element?" (Students respond with answer.)
  - "What does this element say?" (Students respond with answer.)
  - "Say its sound with me." (Students respond with answer.)
  - "Say it by yourselves." (Students respond with answer.)
- Repeat this modeling and practice together multiple times. Keep it quick and to the point.

Step 2: Group Practice of the New Phonetic Element
- Elicit individual and group responses for practice. For example:
  - "Everyone say the letters in this element." (Students respond with answer.)
  - "Say the sound(s) in this element." (Students respond with answer.)
  - "Girls, say its sound"; "Boys, say its sound"; etc.
- Write three of the lesson words containing the new element on the board, on an overhead, or with magnetic letters. Underline the new element in the first word. Say:
  - "What letters are these?" (Students respond with answer.)
  - "What do these letters say?" (Students respond with answer.)
  - Point to the word and say, "What does this word say?" (Students respond with answer.)
  - "Say this word slowly," and drag your finger under the word. (Students respond with answer.)
  - "What word?" (Students respond with answer.)
  - Repeat this procedure with the second and third words.

- Using the three words on the board again, follow this procedure:
  - Point to the underlined element and say, "What element?" (Students respond with answer.)
  - "What word?" (Students respond with answer.)
  - Conduct this activity quickly by calling on individual students and the group for responses.
- Write three additional words on the board, only two of which contain the phonetic element being taught. Underline any two letters in the "non-example" word and ask:
  - "Does this say ____?" (Students should respond, "no.") Move to the next word, which contains the phonetic element being taught.
  - Ask again, "Does this say ____?" (Students should respond, "yes.")
  - "What does this say?" (Students respond with answer.)
  - "Say the word slowly." (Students respond with answer.)
  - "Say the word fast." (Students respond with answer.)
  - Move on to the third word, which contains the phonetic element being taught, and follow the same procedure.
- Review the words on the board by having students say the element first and then the whole word. Do this quickly.
- Make the words containing the element with magnetic letters on the board. Slide the letters of the element in and out of the word, and have students say the element's sound and then the whole word. Students can write the words on their white boards, underline the element in each word, and whisper-read each word.

Step 3: Independent Practice of the New Phonetic Element

- Reinforce the new phonetic element daily with a quick, focused practice session using magnetic letters, flash cards, or white boards. For example:
  - "Show me the letters that say ____ and write those letters three times on your white boards."
- Continue reviewing the new phonetic element for the next few days until students have reached automatic and accurate fluency. Keep the practice sessions quick and to the point.
- Begin partner-practice and group-practice of the *Phonetic Elements Fluency Building Sheets* at this time. You may want to be the "partner" of some students in order to assess the independence of their learning of the particular phonetic element.

Step 4: Review of Phonetic Elements

- Incorporate phonetic elements previously taught—along with a new phonetic element—into a daily quick, focused practice session.
- Use transparencies of previously presented lessons and ask students to choral-read lines by alternating rows of material (e.g., girls read one row, then boys read the next row; the left side of the class reads one row, then the right side of the class reads the next row).
- Read *Decodable Short-Vowel and Long-Vowel Stories* (see *Fluency Building Sheets*) that focus on the targeted phonetic elements. The decodable stories may be used as review or extension activities to reinforce targeted phonetic elements in a teacher-led, small-group setting. Instructional options:

- Choral-read a story with students. After the teacher reads a sentence, have students "echo" read the same sentence.
- Read a story aloud, and omit targeted words for students to verbally fill in.
- Divide students into partnerships or groups and have them take turns reading alternate story sentences.
- Have students individually whisper-read a story while the teacher monitors their reading.

Using the Phonetic Elements Fluency Building Sheets

- Introduce the phonetic element with direct instruction using the *Phonetic Elements Fluency Building Sheets.*
- Model the first two lines and then have students repeat them.
- Model the phonetic element words and have students repeat them in an "echo" fashion.
- Have students whisper-read a fluency sheet to themselves, marking the point at which they stopped when the one-minute timer sounds. Have students record their scores on a *Phonetic Elements Record Graph* (see *Appendix*), which they should store in a folder.
- Instruct students to continue going back to the top of the fluency sheet and then whisper-reading across each row until the bottom row is completed *accurately* in one minute or less.
- Train a student peer to be a "checker." The checker's job is to listen to a student read the fluency sheet and give an OK when the student can read it correctly in one minute or less. The student must "check out" with the teacher before moving on to the next fluency sheet. (The teacher listens to the student read the fluency sheet to determine if the student is 100% accurate in one minute or less.)

Partner Practice:
- Assign partners based on assessment results.
- Train partners in the *Six-Minute Solution Primary* fluency concept (see *Chapter 3*).
- Provide time each day for partner practice with *Phonetic Elements Fluency Building Sheets.* Have students record their scores on the *Phonetic Elements Record Graph* in their folders.

Small-Group Practice:
- Assign students to practice groups based on their assessment results.
- Introduce the phonetic elements on the fluency sheet and have each group quietly "echo" each element. Student groups can then chant the entire fluency sheet together, moving to the next element at the sound of a tap made by the teacher.
- Form partnerships within each small group by having students take turns practicing the fluency sheet with the student sitting next to him/her.
- Number the students within each group, and direct the number 1 students to read the first line, the number 2 students to read the second line, and so on, down the fluency sheet.
- Divide each group, and direct the first half to read the first six lines of a fluency sheet and the second half to read the last six lines.

- Organize the small groups in a variety of ways (e.g., boys only, girls only, alphabetically by name, wearing the color green today) so that students have fun practicing phonetic elements.

Other Instructional Activities/Suggestions for Using the *Phonetic Elements Fluency Building Sheets*

- Using pictures cut out of old magazines, have students make a "Short 'a' Book" (or a book about any other phonetic element they are practicing). Students write the phonetic element at the top of a sheet of paper and paste magazine pictures of objects whose spellings contain that particular phonetic element. (This is also an excellent homework activity.)
- Organize an "element word hunt" in which students look through books for words that have the phonetic element they are practicing. Students list the book's title, the word(s), the page number where they found the word(s), and present a group or class "share-out" of the words they found.
- Time students individually to ensure that they have the phonetic elements down to an automatic level. The goal should be to correctly pronounce 60 words they are practicing within one minute. Record student scores on the *Phonetic Elements Record Graph* in their folders.
- Send the *Phonetic Elements Fluency Building Sheets* home for parents to help their children build phonetic element recognition to an automatic level. **Note:** It is important that students go home knowing how to correctly pronounce the phonetic elements. The sole purpose of the "homework" is to build *recognition fluency* of words containing the specific phonetic elements.

CHAPTER 11

Building Automatic Words Fluency

The *Automatic Words Fluency Building Sheets* (*Primary Automatic Words by Tens*) (see *Fluency Building Sheets*) contain the most frequently encountered sight words in reading texts. They were selected from *The American Heritage Word Frequency Book* (Carroll, Davies, & Richman, 1971), a compilation of the most frequently used words in the English language.

Since students will encounter these words repeatedly when reading, they need to know them to an automatic level. The *Automatic Words Fluency Building Sheets* are organized into 25 numbered lists, with six sets of the same ten words in each list. The sheets can be used to build fluency at the single-word level and to increase sight-word recognition.

Introduction of Unknown Automatic Words

Materials:
- One flash card for each word on the targeted list
- A pocket chart to hold flash cards
- White boards
- Dry-erase markers
- Magnetic letters and small magnetic surfaces
- Large metal rings for holding student-made flash cards

Lesson Format
Day 1—Presentation of the First Group of New Automatic Words
Introduce five of the set of ten words to students on one day, and the remaining five words of the set on the next day.
Step 1: Present the New Automatic Words
- Introduce each of today's five words by using a flash card. Say:
  - "This word is _____ . What word?" (Students respond with answer.)
  - "Say the letters in this word with me." (All spell the sight word.)
  - "What do these letters spell?" (Students respond with answer.)
  - "Say the word again with me." (Students respond with answer.)
- Follow the above format to introduce each of the first five words.
- Place the flash cards in a pocket chart and point to them as all students chant them.
Step 2: Practice of the New Automatic Words
- Hold up one flash card and ask students to read the word.
- Ask students to spell the word with magnetic letters, then to touch each letter and say the word.
- Direct students to scramble the magnetic letters and then quickly spell the word again, touching each letter and saying the word when finished.
- Repeat this sequence with each of the four remaining words. Conduct this activity quickly, and keep students focused.
- Hold up one flash card and ask students to read the word. Then, using the flash card as a model, tell students to write the word on their white boards in a variety of ways (e.g., "write it in uppercase letters"; "write it in lowercase letters"; "write it in all four corners of your white board";

"write it in two corners of your white board"). Repeat with each of the first five new words.

Note: All of the above steps are typically completed in one day.

Day 2—Presentation of the Second Group of New Automatic Words

- Quickly review yesterday's five words via the pocket chart and flash cards.
- Introduce the remaining five words in the set by following **Steps 1** and **2** above.
- Pass out an *Automatic Words Fluency Building Sheet* to the class and lead students in saying all ten words on the first two lines. Follow the "I say it, you say it" format. Chant all ten words together.
- Call on students to read single lines on the fluency sheet. Review any words that students have difficulty remembering.

Step 3: Review of Automatic Words

- Incorporate previously used flash cards with recently learned flash cards to conduct a quick review.
- Have students make their own flash cards, string them on large rings, and practice the word rings with their partners.
- Have students use their flash cards as models, making the words with magnetic letters, mixing up the letters, making the words again, and saying each word.
- Place previously learned flash cards in a pile, facedown in the middle of a small table. Instruct students to draw a flash card and read it. If a student says the word correctly, the student keeps the card and play moves to the next student. If the next students says the word incorrectly, the flash card is returned to the pile, facedown, and play continues with the next student.
- Play whole-group or small-group games (e.g., a "reading bee" instead of a spelling bee) with flash cards.
- Engage students in a "word hunt" for their sets of ten words in previously read books. Students list the book's title, the words, and the page numbers where they found the words.

Partner Practice:

- Assign partners based on assessment results.
- Train students in the *Six-Minute Solution Primary* fluency concept (see *Chapter 3*).
- Provide time each day for partner practice with *Automatic Words Fluency Building Sheets*.
- Have partners record their own scores on an *Automatic Words Record Graph* (see *Appendix*).

Building Automatic Words Fluency With the *Six-Minute Solution Primary* Fluency Concept

Repeated, timed partner readings of assigned lists of automatic words is an excellent way to build students' automatic word knowledge in only six minutes a day. When students can accurately read their assigned list of automatic words at 60 cwpm, they should be moved to the next list of automatic words, with the introduction, instruction, and practice cycle begun all over again. The six-minute peer partnership format is a quick and efficient way to build students' automatic-word vocabulary with very little impact on instructional time.

More Than Six Minutes a Day

One of the advantages of the *Six-Minute Solution Primary* fluency partner model is that students are able to increase their oral reading fluency in only six minutes of an instructional period. The *Six-Minute Solution Primary*'s original grouping configuration is a partnership match based on instructional reading and fluency levels. By utilizing this configuration, the partnership is self-supporting—each partner's reading level mirrors the other's level. In this way, partnerships can function independently with minimal supervision.

However, there might be times when more than six minutes a day must be devoted to fluency practice, as in the following situations:

- On the first day of the week—when partnerships receive new *Phonetic Elements Fluency Building Sheets*, *Automatic Words Fluency Building Sheets*, or *Practice Passages*—more time will be required. Each student in the partnership silently reads the entire phonetic elements sheet, automatic words sheet, or practice passage. If any words are unknown, students consult first with their partners. If neither partner knows a word, the teacher supplies the correct pronunciation.
- Although the program can be easily implemented in a class of struggling readers, an individual fluency program may be more appropriate for some students. In these cases, additional time will be needed for fluency practice.
- Certain grouping configurations, such as guided reading groups, require more than six minutes a day.
- Incorporating additional comprehension activities and/or summary writing will require additional time.

SIX MINUTE

Assessment

Phonetic Elements Assessment

The six subtests of the Phonetic Elements Assessment were designed to accurately assess various phonetic elements that a primary-grade reader would be expected to know. The subtests are organized in a hierarchical order and follow the expected progression found at the primary levels.

The subtests of this assessment must be administered on a one-to-one basis. They may be conducted by a teacher, paraprofessional, or trained parent volunteer.

Assessment Procedure:

1. Make two copies of the Student Copy version of the selected assessment subtest—one for the student and one for the examiner—onto sheets of cardstock or other sturdy paper. Laminate both assessment subtests or place them in plastic sleeves in order to provide the examiner and students with multiple uses of the assessment.
2. Make one copy of the Teacher Record Sheet for each student being assessed.
3. Instruct the student to give the sound or read the elements being assessed. **Do not allow the student more than three seconds per assessment item.** You are assessing for *automatic knowledge of phonemic elements*, which is the goal of this program. Allowing a student too much time to "figure out" each item defeats the purpose of these quick assessments. After three seconds have elapsed, mark the item as incorrect, and instruct the student to move to the next item in the assessment.
4. Mark each assessment item as indicated on the Teacher Record Sheet.
5. Score each student's results on an Individual Comprehensive Phonetic Element Assessment form. This form provides a comprehensive record of all six assessment subtest scores for each student.
6. Based on assessment results, group or partner students for instruction in, and practice with, various phonetic elements. Refer to *Chapter 10* for suggestions on how to enhance your students' phonetic elements proficiency levels.

1. Phonetic Elements Assessment: Letters and Sounds

STUDENT_____ TEACHER _____

PRETEST DATE _____ POSTTEST DATE _____

ASSESSED FOR:

   Letter Names ____   Letter Sounds ____   Names and Sounds ____

- This assessment measures letter/name recognition as well as letter/ sound correspondence.
- In the " + /Response" column:
  - Write a plus sign (+) if the student knows the letter name and/or sound.
  - Leave blank if the student does not know the letter.
  - Write "incorrect response given" if the student responds erroneously.

Letter	+ /Response	Letter	+ /Response
h		j	
m		d	
s		v	
b		f	
g		l	
o		y	
c		k	
r		i	
p		q	
z		t	
e		w	
x		n	
a		u	

1. Phonetic Elements Assessment: Letters and Sounds

Letter	Letter
h	j
m	d
s	v
b	f
g	l
o	y
c	k
r	i
p	q
z	t
e	w
x	n
a	u

1. Phonetic Elements Assessment: Letters and Sounds

TEACHER _____ DATE _____

- Mark an "X" under any unknown letters or sounds.
- Make a folder for each alphabet letter. Place letter/sound sheets in the appropriate folder marked with the name of each student who needs practice with that letter sound.

Student	h	m	s	b	g	o	c	r	p	z	e	x	a	j	d	v	f	l	y	k	i	q	t	w	n	u

2. Phonetic Elements Assessment: CVC Short-Vowel Patterns

STUDENT _____ DATE _____

- In the "+/Response" column:
  - Write a plus sign (+) if the student knows the word.
  - Leave blank if the student does not know the word.
  - Write "incorrect response given" if the student responds erroneously.
- Write the student's total scores in the boxes below the table.

Word	+/Response	Word	+/Response
run		red	
pen		cap	
but		tin	
tan		bed	
mud		gas	
fit		fox	
cab		hen	
man		mob	
hot		rip	
get		hop	

Short "a" Total (5)	Short "e" Total (5)	Short "i" Total (3)	Short "o" Total (4)	Short "u" Total (3)

2. Phonetic Elements Assessment: CVC Short-Vowel Patterns

Word	Word
run	red
pen	cap
but	tin
tan	bed
mud	gas
fit	fox
cab	hen
man	mob
hot	rip
get	hop

2. Phonetic Elements Assessment: CVC Short-Vowel Patterns

- Write the number of words read correctly by each student under the appropriate column heading.

Student	Short "a" (5)	Short "e" (5)	Short "i" (3)	Short "o" (4)	Short "u" (3)

3. Phonetic Elements Assessment: CVC Short-Vowel Patterns—Blends and Digraphs

STUDENT _____ DATE _____

- In the " + /Response" column:
  - Write a plus sign (+) if the student knows the word.
  - Leave blank if the student does not know the word.
  - Write "incorrect response given" if the student responds erroneously.
- Write the student's total scores in the boxes below the table.

Word	+ /Response	Word	+ /Response
plug		quit	
trot		snag	
brat		swim	
twin		then	
grip		sled	
prod		blot	
crab		stem	
glad		flap	
sprig		strap	
club		scab	
throb		chop	
skid		scram	
wham		squid	
split		drug	
smog		shin	
spot		frog	
ring		long	

"r" Blends Total (7)	"l" Blends Total (6)	"s" Blends Total (12)	tw, thr, qu Total (3)	sh, ch, wh, th, ng Digraphs Total (6)

3. Phonetic Elements Assessment: CVC Short-Vowel Patterns—Blends and Digraphs

Word	Word
plug	quit
trot	snag
brat	swim
twin	then
grip	sled
prod	blot
crab	stem
glad	flap
sprig	strap
club	scab
throb	chop
skid	scram
wham	squid
split	drug
smog	shin
spot	frog
ring	long

3. Phonetic Elements Assessment: CVC Short-Vowel Patterns—Blends and Digraphs

- Write the number of words read correctly by each student under the appropriate column heading.

Student	"r" Blends (7)	"l" Blends (6)	"s" Blends (12)	tw, thr, qu (3)	sh, ch, wh, th, ng (6)

4. Phonetic Elements Assessment: Vowel Combinations

STUDENT_____ DATE_____

- In the " + /Response" column:
  - Write a plus sign (+) if the student knows the word.
  - Leave blank if the student does not know the word.
  - Write "incorrect response given" if the student responds erroneously.
- Write the student's total scores in the boxes below the table.

Words	+ /Response	Words	+ /Response
each		peek	
play		paid	
pail		snow	
high		light	
seem		clay	
boat		sigh	
blow		mean	
meat		flown	
wait		soak	
say		keep	
toad		moan	

oa Total (4)	ea Total (3)	ai Total (3)	ow Total (3)	igh Total (3)	ay Total (3)	ee Total (3)

4. Phonetic Elements Assessment:
Vowel Combinations

Words	Words
each	peek
play	paid
pail	snow
high	light
seem	clay
boat	sigh
blow	mean
meat	flown
wait	soak
say	keep
toad	moan

4. Phonetic Elements Assessment:
Vowel Combinations

- Write the number of words read correctly by each student under the appropriate column heading.

Student	oa (4)	ea (3)	ai (3)	ow (3)	igh (3)	ay (3)	ee (3)

5. Phonetic Elements Assessment:
CVCe Combinations With Distractors

STUDENT_____ DATE_____

- In the "+/Response" column:
  - Write a plus sign (+) if the student knows the word.
  - Leave blank if the student does not know the word.
  - Write "incorrect response given" if the student responds erroneously.
- Write the student's total scores in the boxes below the table.

Words	+/Response	Words	+/Response
wipe		pet	
nose		gate	
not		bug	
mile		cube	
case		fog	
Pete		vote	
cake		bite	
bone		cane	
set		mad	
rode		yule	
scene		cute	
dime		hate	
mule		us	
can		home	
him		lime	
five		bit	
made		fuse	
use		Crete	
sale		note	

a_e Total (7)	e_e Total (3)	i_e Total (6)	o_e Total (6)	u_e Total (6)
Short "a" Total (2)	Short "e" Total (2)	Short "i" Total (2)	Short "o" Total (2)	Short "u" Total (2)

5. Phonetic Elements Assessment:
CVCe Combinations With Distractors

Words	Words
wipe	pet
nose	gate
not	bug
mile	cube
case	fog
Pete	vote
cake	bite
bone	cane
set	mad
rode	yule
scene	cute
dime	hate
mule	us
can	home
him	lime
five	bit
made	fuse
use	Crete
sale	note

5. Phonetic Elements Assessment: CVCe Combinations With Distractors

- Write the number of words read correctly by each student under the appropriate column heading.

Student	a_e (7)	e_e (3)	i_e (6)	o_e (6)	u_e (6)	Short "a" (2)	Short "e" (2)	Short "i" (2)	Short "o" (2)	Short "u" (2)

6. Phonetic Elements Assessment: "r" Controlled Vowels With Distractors

STUDENT_____ DATE_____

- In the " + /Response" column:
  - Write a plus sign (+) if the student knows the word.
  - Leave blank if the student does not know the word.
  - Write "incorrect response given" if the student responds erroneously.
- Write the student's total scores in the boxes below the table.

Word	+ /Response	Word	+ /Response
art		girl	
for		bus	
stir		dirt	
mop		hurt	
burn		worn	
arch		blur	
verb		perch	
harm		trap	
firm		star	
stern		bell	
hot		herd	
bird		lit	
curb		cork	
get		duck	
park		firm	
port		fish	
jerk		cord	
curl		ran	

er Total (5)	ir Total (6)	ur Total (5)	ar Total (5)	or Total (5)
Short "a" Total (2)	Short "e" Total (2)	Short "i" Total (2)	Short "o" Total (2)	Short "u" Total (2)

6. Phonetic Elements Assessment:
"r" Controlled Vowels With Distractors

Word	Word
art	girl
for	bus
stir	dirt
mop	hurt
burn	worn
arch	blur
verb	perch
harm	trap
firm	star
stern	bell
hot	herd
bird	lit
curb	cork
get	duck
park	firm
port	fish
jerk	cord
curl	ran

6. Phonetic Elements Assessment:
"r" Controlled Vowels With Distractors

- Write the number of words read correctly by each student under the appropriate column heading.

Student	er (5)	ir (6)	ur (5)	ar (5)	or (5)	Short "a" (2)	Short "e" (2)	Short "i" (2)	Short "o" (2)	Short "u" (2)

Individual Comprehensive Phonetic Elements Assessment

STUDENT_____ DATE _____

GRADE _____ TEACHER _____

1. Letters and Sounds		2. CVC Short-Vowel Patterns		3. CVC Short-Vowel Patterns— Blends and Digraphs		4. Vowel Combinations		5. CVCe Combinations With Distractors		6. "r" Controlled Vowels With Distractors	
h	j	run	red	plug	quit	each	peek	wipe	pet	art	girl
m	d	pen	cap	trot	snag	play	paid	nose	gate	for	bus
s	v	but	tin	brat	swim	pail	snow	not	bug	stir	dirt
b	f	tan	bed	twin	then	high	light	mile	cube	mop	hurt
g	l	mud	gas	grip	sled	seem	clay	case	fog	burn	worn
o	y	fit	fox	prod	blot	boat	sigh	Pete	vote	arch	blur
c	k	cab	hen	crab	stem	blow	mean	cake	bite	verb	perch
r	i	man	mob	glad	flap	meat	flown	bone	cane	harm	trap
p	q	hot	rip	sprig	strap	wait	soak	set	mad	firm	star
z	t	get	hop	club	scab	say	keep	rode	yule	stern	bell
e	w			throb	chop	toad	moan	scene	cute	hot	herd
x	n			skid	scram			dime	hate	bird	lit
a	u			wham	squid			mule	us	curb	cork
				split	drug			can	home	get	duck
				smog	shin			him	lime	park	firm
				spot	frog			five	bit	port	fish
				ring	long			made	fuse	jerk	cord
								use	Crete	curl	ran
								sale	note		
/ 26		/ 20		/ 34		/ 22		/ 38		/ 36	

Primary Automatic Words by Tens

STUDENT _____ DATE _____

- Draw a line through any word the student does not recognize, or reads incorrectly, within three seconds. Non-immediate self-corrections are also counted as errors.
- Record the number of errors at the bottom of each list.

List 1	List 2	List 3	List 4
the	for	this	which
of	it	had	one
and	with	not	you
to	as	are	were
a	his	but	her
in	on	from	all
that	be	or	she
is	at	have	there
was	by	an	would
he	I	they	their
Errors:	Errors:	Errors:	Errors:

List 5	List 6	List 7	List 8
we	out	can	then
him	so	only	do
been	said	other	first
has	what	new	any
when	up	some	my
who	its	time	now
will	about	could	such
more	into	these	like
no	than	two	our
if	them	may	over
Errors:	Errors:	Errors:	Errors:

STUDENT _____ DATE _____

List 9	List 10	List 11	List 12
man	must	should	us
me	through	because	state
even	back	each	good
most	years	just	very
made	where	those	make
after	much	people	world
also	your	Mr.	still
did	way	how	see
many	well	too	own
before	down	little	men
Errors:	Errors:	Errors:	Errors:

List 13	List 14	List 15	List 16
work	day	off	three
long	same	come	himself
here	another	since	few
get	know	go	house
both	year	against	use
between	while	came	during
life	last	right	without
being	might	states	again
under	great	used	place
never	old	take	American
Errors:	Errors:	Errors:	Errors:

STUDENT _____ DATE _____

List 17	List 18	List 19	List 20
around	once	left	though
however	high	number	less
home	general	course	public
small	upon	war	put
found	school	until	think
Mrs.	every	always	almost
thought	don't	away	hand
went	does	something	enough
say	got	fact	far
part	united	water	look
Errors:	Errors:	Errors:	Errors:

List 21	List 22	List 23	List 24
head	why	knew	let
yet	didn't	city	room
government	know	next	president
system	eyes	program	side
set	find	business	social
better	going	give	present
told	look	group	given
nothing	asked	toward	several
night	later	days	order
end	point	young	national
Errors:	Errors:	Errors:	Errors:

STUDENT _____ DATE _____

List 25
second
possible
rather
per
face
among
form
important
often
things
Errors:

Primary Automatic Words by Tens

List 1	List 2	List 3	List 4
the	for	this	which
of	it	had	one
and	with	not	you
to	as	are	were
a	his	but	her
in	on	from	all
that	be	or	she
is	at	have	there
was	by	an	would
he	I	they	their

List 5	List 6	List 7	List 8
we	out	can	then
him	so	only	do
been	said	other	first
has	what	new	any
when	up	some	my
who	its	time	now
will	about	could	such
more	into	these	like
no	than	two	our
if	them	may	over

Primary Automatic Words by Tens (continued)

List 9	List 10	List 11	List 12
man	must	should	us
me	through	because	state
even	back	each	good
most	years	just	very
made	where	those	make
after	much	people	world
also	your	Mr.	still
did	way	how	see
many	well	too	own
before	down	little	men

List 13	List 14	List 15	List 16
work	day	off	three
long	same	come	himself
here	another	since	few
get	know	go	house
both	year	against	use
between	while	came	during
life	last	right	without
being	might	states	again
under	great	used	place
never	old	take	American

Primary Automatic Words by Tens (continued)

List 17	List 18	List 19	List 20
around	once	left	though
however	high	number	less
home	general	course	public
small	upon	war	put
found	school	until	think
Mrs.	every	always	almost
thought	don't	away	hand
went	does	something	enough
say	got	fact	far
part	united	water	look

List 21	List 22	List 23	List 24
head	why	knew	let
yet	didn't	city	room
government	know	next	president
system	eyes	program	side
set	find	business	social
better	going	give	present
told	look	group	given
nothing	asked	toward	several
night	later	days	order
end	point	young	national

Primary Automatic Words by Tens (continued)

List 25
second
possible
rather
per
face
among
form
important
often
things

Primary Automatic Words by Tens

- Record student names in the first column.
- Mark an "X" under the list number that indicates the starting instructional level for each student.

STUDENT	LIST NUMBER																								
	1	2	3	4	5	6	7	8	9	10	11	12	13	14	15	16	17	18	19	20	21	22	23	24	25

Birds: Our Feathered Friends

0	There are thousands of different birds. Birds have two
9	legs and two wings. Some birds are very small. Others
19	are large. Birds are the only animals that have feathers.
29	Feathers can be any color. They keep birds warm and dry.
40	Flight feathers are very smooth.
45	Most birds can fly. Birds can fly because they have
55	very light bones. Their strong muscles move the wings.
64	The tail helps the bird to steer in the sky. Different birds
76	have different shaped wings. This is because birds live in
86	different places. Most birds live in trees. Other birds live
96	high in the hills. Some live on the ground. Some birds fly
108	long distances. They live one place in the summer. They
118	live someplace else in the winter.
124	Some birds cannot fly. They are too big. The biggest
134	bird is an ostrich. It can grow to be 8 feet tall and can
148	weigh 300 pounds. An ostrich has strong legs. It can run
159	very fast. Some birds are good swimmers. Penguins are
168	birds that can swim. They can swim very fast. They use
179	their wings to swim.
183	

Total Words Read _____

– Errors _____

= CWPM _____

Fish Facts

0	There are many kinds of fish. They come in many
10	colors, shapes, and sizes. Some fish are as small as
20	tadpoles. Others are larger than crocodiles. Some fish are
29	thin, while others are fat.
34	All fish have three important things in common. They
43	all live in water. All fish have fins to control the direction
55	of their movement. They all use gills to get oxygen from
66	the water.
68	Some fish live in the ocean. They are saltwater
77	fish. Other fish live in rivers and lakes. These fish are
88	freshwater fish.
90	Fish are good swimmers. They propel themselves
97	through the water by moving their tails from side to side.
108	Fish use their fins to steer. Some fish have only one fin.
120	But most fish have more than one fin.
128	Gills are water-breathing organs. They are located
136	in the fish's mouth. The fish takes in water through its
147	mouth. The water goes through gill slits. These help the
157	fish to get oxygen from the water as it passes through.
168	

Total Words Read _____

− Errors _____

= CWPM _____

Reptiles: Cold-Blooded Animals

0   Reptiles have lived on earth for a long time. They

10 have been here for more than 300 million years. Reptiles

20 are animals. They are cold-blooded. This means that their

30 body temperature changes. When it is cold outside, reptiles

39 are cold. When it is hot outside, reptiles are hot. Reptiles

50 eat 30 to 50 times less food than mammals. This is because

62 they do not have to burn fuel for energy. Reptiles have dry,

74 scaly skin. Their skin protects them from drying out.

83   There are many kinds of reptiles. More than 8,000

92 types of reptiles live on earth. Reptiles live all over the

103 world. Some reptiles live on land. Others live in the water.

114 Living reptiles fall into four classes. Turtles are one class

124 of reptiles. They are reptiles with a shell. Turtles are the

135 oldest living reptile group. Crocodiles are another class of

144 reptiles. Alligators are included in this group. Lizards are

153 a type of reptile. Snakes are reptiles, too.

161

Total Words Read _____

– Errors _____

= CWPM _____

San Diego Quick Assessment of Reading Ability

Directions: This is an individually administered sight-word reading assessment. Because this is a measure of sight-word knowledge, students need to recognize the words very quickly. Give a copy of the Student Form to the student to read. Choose a word list that is two to three grade levels below the student's current grade level as the starting point. Ask the student to read each word aloud. Keep the student moving down the lists. Do not allow more than three to five seconds on any word. Rather, tell the student to go on to the next word. Mark the word skipped as incorrect. Stop the assessment when the student has missed three or more words in a list. Record the highest grade level for each of the three levels (independent, instructional, and frustration) in the Errors & Reading Levels table when testing is completed.

ERRORS & READING LEVELS

Student Name	Reading Level		
	Independent (1 error)	Instructional (2 errors)	Frustration (3+ errors)

San Diego Quick Assessment of Reading Ability

NAME: _____ DATE: _____

Record the highest grade level for each:

INDEPENDENT _____ INSTRUCTIONAL _____ FRUSTRATION _____

Preprimer		Grade Three		Grade Seven		Grade Eleven	
see	____	city	____	amber	____	galore	____
play	____	middle	____	dominion	____	rotunda	____
me	____	moment	____	sundry	____	capitalism	____
at	____	frightened	____	capillary	____	prevaricate	____
run	____	exclaimed	____	impetuous	____	visible	____
go	____	several	____	blight	____	exonerate	____
and	____	lonely	____	wrest	____	superannuate	____
look	____	drew	____	enumerate	____	luxuriate	____
can	____	since	____	daunted	____	piebald	____
here	____	straight	____	condescend	____	crunch	____

Primer		Grade Four		Grade Eight	
you	____	decided	____	capacious	____
come	____	served	____	limitation	____
not	____	amazed	____	pretext	____
with	____	silent	____	intrigue	____
jump	____	wrecked	____	delusion	____
help	____	improved	____	immaculate	____
is	____	certainly	____	ascent	____
work	____	entered	____	acrid	____
are	____	realized	____	binocular	____
this	____	interrupted	____	embankment	____

Grade One		Grade Five		Grade Nine	
road	____	scanty	____	conscientious	____
live	____	business	____	isolation	____
thank	____	develop	____	molecule	____
when	____	considered	____	ritual	____
bigger	____	discussed	____	momentous	____
how	____	behaved	____	vulnerable	____
always	____	splendid	____	kinship	____
night	____	acquainted	____	conservatism	____
spring	____	escaped	____	jaunty	____
today	____	grim	____	inventive	____

Grade Two		Grade Six		Grade Ten	
our	____	bridge	____	zany	____
please	____	commercial	____	jerkin	____
myself	____	abolish	____	nausea	____
town	____	trucker	____	gratuitous	____
early	____	apparatus	____	linear	____
send	____	elementary	____	inept	____
wide	____	comment	____	legality	____
believe	____	necessity	____	aspen	____
quietly	____	gallery	____	amnesty	____
carefully	____	relativity	____	barometer	____

From "The Graded Word List: Quick Gauge of Reading Ability" by Margaret LaPray, Helen Ross, and Raman Royal, in *Journal of Reading*, 12, 305–307 (January, 1969) Copyright © by Margaret LaPray and the International Reading Association. All rights reserved. Reprinted with permission.

San Diego Quick Assessment of Reading Ability

see	exclaimed	daunted
play	several	condescend
me	lonely	capacious
at	drew	limitation
run	since	pretext
go	straight	intrigue
and	decided	delusion
look	served	immaculate
can	amazed	ascent
here	silent	acrid
you	wrecked	binocular
come	improved	embankment
not	certainly	conscientious
with	entered	isolation
jump	realized	molecule
help	interrupted	ritual
is	scanty	momentous
work	business	vulnerable
are	develop	kinship
this	considered	conservatism
road	discussed	jaunty
live	behaved	inventive
thank	splendid	zany
when	acquainted	jerkin
bigger	escaped	nausea
how	grim	gratuitous
always	bridge	linear
night	commercial	inept
spring	abolish	legality
today	trucker	aspen
our	apparatus	amnesty
please	elementary	barometer
myself	comment	galore
town	necessity	rotunda
early	gallery	capitalism
send	relativity	prevaricate
wide	amber	visible
believe	dominion	exonerate
quietly	sundry	superannuate
carefully	capillary	luxuriate
city	impetuous	piebald
middle	blight	crunch
moment	wrest	
frightened	enumerate	

SIX MINUTE

Fluency Building Sheets

Short a and Short i Letter Sounds

(Sounds only or letters and sounds together)

0	i	a	a	i	i
5	a	a	i	i	a
10	a	i	a	i	a
15	i	a	a	i	a
20	i	i	i	a	a
25	a	a	a	a	i
30	i	a	i	a	i
35	a	i	a	i	a
40	i	a	a	i	i
45	a	i	a	i	a
50	i	a	i	a	i
55	a	a	i	a	i
60					

Short a, Short i, and Short o Letter Sounds
(Sounds only or letters and sounds together)

0	o	o	a	i	o
5	o	a	a	i	i
10	o	o	o	a	i
15	a	i	o	o	i
20	o	a	i	o	a
25	i	i	o	a	i
30	o	a	i	o	o
35	o	a	i	o	a
40	i	o	a	a	o
45	o	i	a	o	o
50	o	i	i	a	a
55	o	a	i	o	o
60					

Short a, Short i, Short o, and Short u Letter Sounds
(Sounds only or letters and sounds together)

0	u	a	i	u	o
5	a	u	u	i	i
10	i	u	a	o	i
15	u	a	i	i	o
20	a	u	i	u	u
25	u	i	a	a	u
30	a	i	u	u	o
35	u	i	u	a	o
40	u	a	i	o	u
45	i	u	o	a	u
50	a	i	o	u	u
55	o	i	u	a	u
60					

Short a, Short e, Short i, Short o, and Short u Letter Sounds

(Sounds only or letters and sounds together)

0	e	o	i	e	u
5	i	o	e	e	a
10	e	u	i	a	i
15	e	e	a	u	u
20	o	u	e	i	u
25	a	i	e	u	u
30	i	e	o	a	u
35	u	e	e	o	e
40	a	e	i	o	u
45	e	a	o	e	u
50	e	i	a	u	o
55	o	e	i	e	u
60					

Consonants f, g, l

(Sounds only or letters and sounds together)

0	g	l	f	g	g
5	g	f	l	g	f
10	f	l	f	f	g
15	l	l	f	g	g
20	l	f	g	f	l
25	f	g	l	f	g
30	l	g	f	f	l
35	g	l	f	g	l
40	f	l	f	g	g
45	l	f	l	l	g
50	f	g	g	l	g
55	g	l	l	f	l
60					

Consonants b, c, t

(Sounds only or letters and sounds together)

0	b	c	t	t	c
5	t	c	c	b	t
10	c	c	t	b	b
15	c	t	b	c	t
20	t	c	c	b	t
25	c	b	t	c	b
30	t	c	t	t	b
35	c	b	c	c	t
40	c	c	b	t	c
45	t	c	b	b	c
50	c	c	t	t	b
55	t	c	b	c	t
60					

Consonants h, m, p
(Sounds only or letters and sounds together)

0	m	p	h	h	m
5	p	h	m	m	p
10	p	m	p	m	h
15	h	h	m	m	p
20	m	h	h	p	p
25	h	h	m	m	p
30	p	h	p	m	p
35	m	h	m	p	h
40	h	p	m	m	p
45	p	h	h	m	h
50	h	p	h	m	p
55	m	m	h	p	m
60					

Consonants d, r, w
(Sounds only or letters and sounds together)

0	d	w	r	r	d
5	r	d	d	w	w
10	r	w	d	r	d
15	d	d	r	w	w
20	r	d	w	d	d
25	w	d	w	r	d
30	r	r	w	w	d
35	d	r	w	d	w
40	r	d	r	w	r
45	d	w	d	w	d
50	r	d	d	w	r
55	w	w	d	r	w
60					

Consonants k, n, z
(Sounds only or letters and sounds together)

0	k	n	n	k	z
5	k	z	z	n	k
10	z	n	n	k	k
15	n	z	k	n	z
20	k	k	n	n	n
25	n	z	k	k	n
30	z	z	k	n	n
35	n	z	n	z	k
40	k	n	n	z	z
45	n	k	z	k	k
50	z	z	k	n	n
55	z	k	n	k	z
60					

Consonants j, s, y
(Sounds only or letters and sounds together)

0	y	s	j	j	s
5	s	s	j	y	j
10	s	j	y	y	s
15	j	j	s	s	y
20	y	s	j	y	s
25	y	j	j	y	y
30	j	s	j	y	j
35	s	j	y	y	j
40	s	s	y	s	s
45	j	j	y	s	y
50	y	s	y	j	j
55	j	s	j	u	j
60					

Consonants q, v, x
(Sounds only or letters and sounds together)

0	q	x	v	q	v
5	x	x	q	q	x
10	v	v	q	x	q
15	q	v	v	x	v
20	v	x	v	x	q
25	x	q	x	q	v
30	q	q	x	v	x
35	v	v	x	x	q
40	x	q	v	x	q
45	q	v	v	x	q
50	v	q	q	v	v
55	q	v	q	x	x
60					

VC Pattern Fluency Sheet

0	am	ax	as	an	at
5	in	it	if	is	on
10	of	ox	Ed	us	up
15	am	ax	as	an	at
20	in	it	if	is	on
25	of	ox	Ed	us	up
30	am	ax	as	an	at
35	in	it	if	is	on
40	of	ox	Ed	us	up
45	am	ax	as	an	at
50	in	it	if	is	on
55	of	ox	Ed	us	up
60					

VC Pattern Fluency Sheet

0	at	am	it	an	if
5	up	in	is	on	us
10	as	ox	Ed	of	ax
15	at	am	it	an	if
20	up	in	is	on	us
25	as	ox	Ed	of	ax
30	at	am	it	an	if
35	up	in	is	on	us
40	as	ox	Ed	of	ax
45	at	am	it	an	if
50	up	in	is	on	us
55	as	ox	Ed	of	ax
60					

CVC Pattern Fluency Sheet

0	cat	ram	sat	Dan	rat
5	cap	bag	jam	sat	rag
10	mad	bat	tag	ran	fan
15	can	fat	nap	man	Sam
20	cat	ram	sat	Dan	rat
25	cap	bag	jam	sat	rag
30	mad	bat	tag	ran	fan
35	can	fat	nap	man	Sam
40	cat	ram	sat	Dan	rat
45	cap	bag	jam	sat	rag
50	mad	bat	tag	ran	fan
55	can	fat	nap	man	Sam
60					

CVC Pattern Fluency Sheet

0	jam	pan	lap	mad	nag
5	rag	tap	van	cab	dad
10	sad	ham	rat	mad	man
15	wag	gas	sap	tan	yap
20	pad	ran	map	fat	has
25	jam	pan	lap	mad	nag
30	rag	tap	van	cab	dad
35	sad	ham	rat	mad	man
40	wag	gas	sap	tan	yap
45	pad	ran	map	fat	has
50	jam	pan	lap	mad	nag
55	rag	tap	van	cab	dad
60					

CCVC Pattern Fluency Sheet

0	brag	crab	drag	grab	slam
5	tram	brat	clap	flag	glad
10	slap	trap	brad	clam	flat
15	scab	bran	snap	swam	plan
20	brag	crab	drag	grab	slam
25	tram	brat	clap	flag	glad
30	slap	trap	brad	clam	flat
35	scab	bran	snap	swam	plan
40	brag	crab	drag	grab	slam
45	tram	brat	clap	flag	glad
50	slap	trap	brad	clam	flat
55	scab	bran	snap	swam	plan
60					

CCVC Pattern Fluency Sheet

0	bran	clam	flap	scan	slap
5	trap	blab	brat	flax	flat
10	flag	clan	slab	cram	scan
15	glad	snag	Stan	slat	plan
20	bran	clam	flap	scan	slap
25	trap	blab	brat	flax	flat
30	flag	clan	slab	cram	scan
35	glad	snag	Stan	slat	plan
40	bran	clam	flap	scan	slap
45	trap	blab	brat	flax	flat
50	flag	clan	slab	cram	scan
55	glad	snag	Stan	slat	plan
60					

CVCC Pattern Fluency Sheet

0	back	camp	fast	gang	hand
5	jack	mast	mask	raft	tack
10	gasp	pack	lamp	last	past
15	sand	task	cast	rack	tank
20	back	camp	fast	gang	hand
25	jack	mast	mask	raft	tack
30	gasp	pack	lamp	last	past
35	sand	task	cast	rack	tank
40	back	camp	fast	gang	hand
45	jack	mast	mask	raft	tack
50	gasp	pack	lamp	last	past
55	sand	task	cast	rack	tank
60					

Mixed Practice Fluency Sheet

0	tag	glad	stab	fast	sag
5	trap	band	cab	task	pack
10	bat	can	flat	blab	camp
15	rag	mask	lamp	wag	ran
20	tag	glad	stab	fast	sag
25	trap	band	cab	task	pack
30	bat	can	flat	blab	camp
35	rag	mask	lamp	wag	ran
40	tag	glad	stab	fast	sag
45	trap	band	cab	task	pack
50	bat	can	flat	blab	camp
55	rag	mask	lamp	wag	ran
60					

CVC Pattern Fluency Sheet

0	big	win	pit	hip	rib
5	did	sit	dig	lip	rid
10	six	dim	kit	tin	fit
15	pig	lid	hip	tip	mix
20	big	win	pit	hip	rib
25	did	sit	dig	lip	rid
30	six	dim	kit	tin	fit
35	pig	lid	hip	tip	mix
40	big	win	pit	hip	rib
45	did	sit	dig	lip	rid
50	six	dim	kit	tin	fit
55	pig	lid	hip	tip	mix
60					

CVC Pattern Fluency Sheet

0	fig	kit	fib	bid	pin
5	rid	bit	lid	jib	dim
10	fin	sit	pit	rig	his
15	him	six	zip	fit	win
20	fig	kit	fib	bid	pin
25	rid	bit	lid	jib	dim
30	fin	sit	pit	rig	his
35	him	six	zip	fit	win
40	fig	kit	fib	bid	pin
45	rid	bit	lid	jib	dim
50	fin	sit	pit	rig	his
55	him	six	zip	fit	win
60					

Discrimination Practice

0	cat	big	win	Dan	rat
5	cap	pit	jam	hip	rag
10	mad	lid	tag	tin	fan
15	can	dim	dig	man	six
20	cat	big	win	Dan	rat
25	cap	pit	jam	hip	rag
30	mad	lid	tag	tin	fan
35	can	dim	dig	man	six
40	cat	big	win	Dan	rat
45	cap	pit	jam	hip	rag
50	mad	lid	tag	tin	fan
55	can	dim	dig	man	six
60					

CCVC Pattern Fluency Sheet

0	slim	skip	spin	drip	skin
5	brig	slip	swim	trip	twig
10	twin	trim	grin	skip	flip
15	grim	grit	trip	spit	slit
20	slim	skip	spin	drip	skin
25	brig	slip	swim	trip	twig
30	twin	trim	grin	skip	flip
35	grim	grit	trip	spit	slit
40	slim	skip	spin	drip	skin
45	brig	slip	swim	trip	twig
50	twin	trim	grin	skip	flip
55	grim	grit	trip	spit	slit
60					

CCVC Pattern Fluency Sheet

0	flit	skin	prim	slit	trip
5	slim	spit	drip	trip	slid
10	grin	skid	twin	slip	brim
15	swig	trim	swim	flip	snip
20	flit	skin	prim	slit	trip
25	slim	spit	drip	trip	slid
30	grin	skid	twin	slip	brim
35	swig	trim	swim	flip	snip
40	flit	skin	prim	slit	trip
45	slim	spit	drip	trip	slid
50	grin	skid	twin	slip	brim
55	swig	trim	swim	flip	snip
60					

CCVC Pattern Fluency Sheet

0	wilt	mint	milk	sing	silk
5	sift	sink	gift	list	lick
10	tilt	mist	king	gift	wind
15	risk	fist	mist	wing	pick
20	wilt	mint	milk	sing	silk
25	sift	sink	gift	list	lick
30	tilt	mist	king	gift	wind
35	risk	fist	mist	wing	pick
40	wilt	mint	milk	sing	silk
45	sift	sink	gift	list	lick
50	tilt	mist	king	gift	wind
55	risk	fist	mist	wing	pick
60					

Mixed Practice Fluency Sheet

0	fin	lick	grip	bib	pick
5	mix	skip	ring	lip	drip
10	rid	gift	grip	trip	win
15	risk	kit	pig	spin	tilt
20	fin	lick	grip	bib	pick
25	mix	skip	ring	lip	drip
30	rid	gift	grip	trip	win
35	risk	kit	pig	spin	tilt
40	fin	lick	grip	bib	pick
45	mix	skip	ring	lip	drip
50	rid	gift	grip	trip	win
55	risk	kit	pig	spin	tilt
60					

Discrimination Practice

0	brag	grin	flip	grab	spit
5	tram	skip	clap	drip	slip
10	slim	brat	drag	trip	slam
15	trim	crab	spin	flag	glad
20	brag	grin	flip	grab	spit
25	tram	skip	clap	drip	slip
30	slim	brat	drag	trip	slam
35	trim	crab	spin	flag	glad
40	brag	grin	flip	grab	spit
45	tram	skip	clap	drip	slip
50	slim	brat	drag	trip	slam
55	trim	crab	spin	flag	glad
60					

CVC Pattern Fluency Sheet

0	bed	web	den	get	leg
5	set	men	beg	ten	red
10	net	fed	yet	pep	yes
15	led	wet	pen	jet	beg
20	bed	web	den	get	leg
25	set	men	beg	ten	red
30	net	fed	yet	pep	yes
35	led	wet	pen	jet	beg
40	bed	web	den	get	leg
45	set	men	beg	ten	red
50	net	fed	yet	pep	yes
55	led	wet	pen	jet	beg
60					

CVC Pattern Fluency Sheet

0	met	red	yes	leg	led
5	hem	get	pep	wed	pen
10	let	leg	pet	bed	hen
15	beg	set	web	den	met
20	met	red	yes	leg	led
25	hem	get	pep	wed	pen
30	let	leg	pet	bed	hen
35	beg	set	web	den	met
40	met	red	yes	leg	led
45	hem	get	pep	wed	pen
50	let	leg	pet	bed	hen
55	beg	set	web	den	met
60					

CCVC Pattern Fluency Sheet

0	sped	prep	fled	stem	bled
5	step	bred	fret	sled	glen
10	Fred	fret	sped	bled	trek
15	sped	prep	fled	stem	bled
20	step	bred	fret	sled	glen
25	Fred	fret	sped	bled	trek
30	sped	prep	fled	stem	bled
35	step	bred	fret	sled	glen
40	Fred	fret	sped	bled	trek
45	sped	prep	fled	stem	bled
50	step	bred	fret	sled	glen
55	Fred	fret	sped	bled	trek
60					

CCVC Pattern Fluency Sheet

0	bred	fret	glen	fled	glen
5	stem	sled	step	stem	fled
10	sped	prep	flex	step	bled
15	sped	sled	trek	Fred	fret
20	bred	fret	glen	fled	glen
25	stem	sled	step	stem	fled
30	sped	prep	flex	step	bled
35	sped	sled	trek	Fred	fret
40	bred	fret	glen	fled	glen
45	stem	sled	step	stem	fled
50	sped	prep	flex	step	bled
55	sped	sled	trek	Fred	fret
60					

CVCC Pattern Fluency Sheet

0	deck	weld	rest	self	left
5	send	help	next	belt	wept
10	dent	nest	went	zest	neck
15	lend	bent	melt	next	neck
20	cent	west	desk	best	sent
25	deck	weld	rest	self	left
30	send	help	next	belt	wept
35	dent	nest	went	zest	neck
40	lend	bent	melt	next	neck
45	cent	west	desk	best	sent
50	deck	weld	rest	self	left
55	send	help	next	belt	wept
60					

Mixed Practice Fluency Sheet

0	led	yes	west	desk	sled
5	jet	rent	desk	pen	felt
10	fled	help	shed	glen	men
15	red	sent	pest	get	pelt
20	yet	step	kept	rest	went
25	led	yes	west	desk	sled
30	jet	rent	desk	pen	felt
35	fled	help	shed	glen	men
40	red	sent	pest	get	pelt
45	yet	step	kept	rest	went
50	led	yes	west	desk	sled
55	jet	rent	desk	pen	felt
60					

CVC Pattern Fluency Sheet

0	top	cot	box	got	mop
5	not	fox	Bob	sod	sob
10	cop	dot	lot	tot	box
15	got	cob	lop	rod	jog
20	mob	nod	hot	bog	rot
25	top	cot	box	got	mop
30	not	fox	Bob	sod	sob
35	cop	dot	lot	tot	box
40	got	cob	lop	rod	jog
45	mob	nod	hot	bog	rot
50	top	cot	box	got	mop
55	not	fox	Bob	sod	sob
60					

CVC Pattern Fluency Sheet

0	cod	job	cop	pop	got
5	cop	nod	rob	hop	rod
10	sob	box	top	mob	fox
15	pod	mob	sod	not	sod
20	Bob	cot	job	lop	top
25	cod	job	cop	pop	got
30	cop	nod	rob	hop	rod
35	sob	box	top	mob	fox
40	pod	mob	sod	not	sod
45	Bob	cot	job	lop	top
50	cod	job	cop	pop	got
55	cop	nod	rob	hop	rod
60					

Discrimination Practice

0	met	fox	Bob	leg	box
5	top	get	cot	mop	pen
10	let	sod	pet	sob	hen
15	hem	pep	got	wed	not
20	red	top	leg	dot	led
25	met	fox	Bob	leg	box
30	top	get	cot	mop	pen
35	let	sod	pet	sob	hen
40	hem	pep	got	wed	not
45	red	top	leg	dot	led
50	met	fox	Bob	leg	box
55	top	get	cot	mop	pen
60					

CCVC Pattern Fluency Sheet

0	blot	trot	spot	crop	clot
5	drop	trod	snob	plod	crop
10	stop	slot	blob	plot	clog
15	flop	prop	prod	slop	glob
20	blot	trot	spot	crop	clot
25	drop	trod	snob	plod	crop
30	stop	slot	blob	plot	clog
35	flop	prop	prod	slop	glob
40	blot	trot	spot	crop	clot
45	drop	trod	snob	plod	crop
50	stop	slot	blob	plot	clog
55	flop	prop	prod	slop	glob
60					

CCVC Pattern Fluency Sheet

0	stop	prod	clot	slop	prop
5	plot	spot	crop	snob	trot
10	trod	glob	prop	blot	drop
15	slop	clod	clot	plod	slot
20	stop	prod	clot	slop	prop
25	plot	spot	crop	snob	trot
30	trod	glob	prop	blot	drop
35	slop	clod	clot	plod	slot
40	stop	prod	clot	slop	prop
45	plot	spot	crop	snob	trot
50	trod	glob	prop	blot	drop
55	slop	clod	clot	plod	slot
60					

CVCC Pattern Fluency Sheet

0	rock	mock	sock	bond	romp
5	fond	pomp	tock	cost	lock
10	lost	sock	dock	pond	lock
15	rock	mock	sock	bond	romp
20	fond	pomp	tock	cost	lock
25	lost	sock	dock	pond	lock
30	rock	mock	sock	bond	romp
35	fond	pomp	tock	cost	lock
40	lost	sock	dock	pond	lock
45	rock	mock	sock	bond	romp
50	fond	pomp	tock	cost	lock
55	lost	sock	dock	pond	lock
60					

Mixed Practice Fluency Sheet

0	stop	pot	mop	sob	cop
5	fond	rock	tot	romp	slob
10	sock	crop	drop	lock	bond
15	pop	not	slop	trot	fox
20	stop	pot	mop	sob	cop
25	fond	rock	tot	romp	slob
30	sock	crop	drop	lock	bond
35	pop	not	slop	trot	fox
40	stop	pot	mop	sob	cop
45	fond	rock	tot	romp	slob
50	sock	crop	drop	lock	bond
55	pop	not	slop	trot	fox
60					

Discrimination Practice

0	rock	left	sock	next	romp
5	help	pomp	deck	lock	sock
10	dock	pond	belt	weld	self
15	mock	send	fond	bond	tock
20	rock	left	sock	next	romp
25	help	pomp	deck	lock	sock
30	dock	pond	belt	weld	self
35	mock	send	fond	bond	tock
40	rock	left	sock	next	romp
45	help	pomp	deck	lock	sock
50	dock	pond	belt	weld	self
55	mock	send	fond	bond	tock
60					

CVC Pattern Fluency Sheet

0	bus	hum	cub	bug	run
5	cup	rug	mud	sum	pup
10	gum	fun	bud	tub	dug
15	rub	dug	sun	gum	bud
20	bus	hum	cub	bug	run
25	cup	rug	mud	sum	pup
30	gum	fun	bud	tub	dug
35	rub	dug	sun	gum	bud
40	bus	hum	cub	bug	run
45	cup	rug	mud	sum	pup
50	gum	fun	bud	tub	dug
55	rub	dug	sun	gum	bud
60					

CVC Pattern Fluency Sheet

0	hug	pup	run	sub	cup
5	mud	nut	rub	cut	gum
10	jug	sun	jut	bun	mum
15	hut	but	mug	cup	tub
20	hug	pup	run	sub	cup
25	mud	nut	rub	cut	gum
30	jug	sun	jut	bun	mum
35	hut	but	mug	cup	tub
40	hug	pup	run	sub	cup
45	mud	nut	rub	cut	gum
50	jug	sun	jut	bun	mum
55	hut	but	mug	cup	tub
60					

Discrimination Practice

0	mad	big	bed	top	bus
5	web	bat	win	cot	hum
10	box	den	tag	pit	fun
15	cub	got	get	ran	hip
20	fit	leg	mop	bug	fan
25	cat	rib	set	run	fox
30	not	rat	did	men	fun
35	cup	beg	bag	sit	dog
40	rug	sob	ten	man	dig
45	red	mud	dot	six	rag
50	nap	lip	fed	lot	pup
55	gum	jam	rid	net	jog
60					

CCVC Pattern Fluency Sheet

0	spun	grub	club	drum	slum
5	slug	snub	glum	plus	plum
10	spud	grub	stub	stun	plug
15	scum	crud	swum	snub	snug
20	spun	grub	club	drum	slum
25	slug	snub	glum	plus	plum
30	spud	grub	stub	stun	plug
35	scum	crud	swum	snub	snug
40	spun	grub	club	drum	slum
45	slug	snub	glum	plus	plum
50	spud	grub	stub	stun	plug
55	scum	crud	swum	snub	snug
60					

CCVC Pattern Fluency Sheet

0	slug	club	snub	plum	smug
5	stub	glum	plus	drum	drug
10	spun	stub	snug	plug	slum
15	grub	slum	spud	glut	stun
20	slug	club	snub	plum	smug
25	stub	glum	plus	drum	drug
30	spun	stub	snug	plug	slum
35	grub	slum	spud	glut	stun
40	slug	club	snub	plum	smug
45	stub	glum	plus	drum	drug
50	spun	stub	snug	plug	slum
55	grub	slum	spud	glut	stun
60					

CCVC Pattern Fluency Sheet

0	just	fund	sung	jump	lump
5	hunk	pump	punt	luck	junk
10	rung	sulk	tusk	hunt	runt
15	rust	bulk	dull	spun	dump
20	just	fund	sung	jump	lump
25	hunk	pump	punt	luck	junk
30	rung	sulk	tusk	hunt	runt
35	rust	bulk	dull	spun	dump
40	just	fund	sung	jump	lump
45	hunk	pump	punt	luck	junk
50	rung	sulk	tusk	hunt	runt
55	rust	bulk	dull	spun	dump
60					

Mixed Practice Fluency Sheet

0	hunt	stun	drum	run	cup
5	hut	duck	dust	pump	dug
10	rung	drug	club	lung	just
15	plug	fun	bus	plus	nut
20	hunt	stun	drum	run	cup
25	hut	duck	dust	pump	dug
30	rung	drug	club	lung	just
35	plug	fun	bus	plus	nut
40	hunt	stun	drum	run	cup
45	hut	duck	dust	pump	dug
50	rung	drug	club	lung	just
55	plug	fun	bus	plus	nut
60					

Discrimination Practice

0	brag	slim	sped	blot	spun
5	trot	crab	skip	fled	club
10	grub	spot	drag	spin	stem
15	drum	crop	step	grab	drip
20	clot	slum	fret	skin	slam
25	tram	brig	sled	drop	slug
30	snob	brat	slip	glen	snub
35	glum	plod	clap	swim	bled
40	plus	trod	trek	flag	trip
45	step	plum	flop	twig	glad
50	slap	twin	prep	prop	spud
55	swum	flat	grin	bred	glob
60					

"ch" Words Fluency Sheet

0	chat	chest	church	inch	rich
5	chin	much	such	chick	chap
10	check	chip	chop	rich	chin
15	bench	lunch	chick	much	ranch
20	chat	chest	church	inch	rich
25	chin	much	such	chick	chap
30	check	chip	chop	rich	chin
35	bench	lunch	chick	much	ranch
40	chat	chest	church	inch	rich
45	chin	much	such	chick	chap
50	check	chip	chop	rich	chin
55	bench	lunch	chick	much	ranch
60					

"ch" Words Fluency Sheet

0	chin	chat	chip	chop	chest
5	chill	chew	chug	chum	chunk
10	chess	chunk	chest	chick	check
15	chin	chat	chip	chop	chest
20	chill	chew	chug	chum	chunk
25	chess	chunk	chest	chick	check
30	chin	chat	chip	chop	chest
35	chill	chew	chug	chum	chunk
40	chess	chunk	chest	chick	check
45	chin	chat	chip	chop	chest
50	chill	chew	chug	chum	chunk
55	chess	chunk	chest	chick	check
60					

"sh" Words Fluency Sheet

0	wish	she	ship	shut	push
5	shell	bush	fish	shop	shot
10	dash	dish	wash	rush	rash
15	cash	shin	rush	ash	mush
20	wish	she	ship	shut	push
25	shell	bush	fish	shop	shot
30	dash	dish	wash	rush	rash
35	cash	shin	rush	ash	mush
40	wish	she	ship	shut	push
45	shell	bush	fish	shop	shot
50	dash	dish	wash	rush	rash
55	cash	shin	rush	ash	mush
60					

"sh" Words Fluency Sheet

0	shot	shut	shack	she	shed
5	shell	ship	shop	shin	shift
10	shy	shall	shelf	shark	short
15	shot	shut	shack	she	shed
20	shell	ship	shop	shin	shift
25	shy	shall	shelf	shark	short
30	shot	shut	shack	she	shed
35	shell	ship	shop	shin	shift
40	shy	shall	shelf	shark	short
45	shot	shut	shack	she	shed
50	shell	ship	shop	shin	shift
55	shy	shall	shelf	shark	short
60					

Voiceless "th" Words Fluency Sheet

0	bath	thank	thing	with	math
5	thin	thick	path	tenth	tooth
10	sixth	thing	think	moth	third
15	booth	both	thumb	fifth	moth
20	bath	thank	thing	with	math
25	thin	thick	path	tenth	tooth
30	sixth	thing	think	moth	third
35	booth	both	thumb	fifth	moth
40	bath	thank	thing	with	math
45	thin	thick	path	tenth	tooth
50	sixth	thing	think	moth	third
55	booth	both	thumb	fifth	moth
60					

Voiced "th" Words Fluency Sheet

0	the	them	than	that	this
5	they	then	these	those	there
10	the	them	than	that	this
15	they	then	these	those	there
20	the	them	than	that	this
25	they	then	these	those	there
30	the	them	than	that	this
35	they	then	these	those	there
40	the	them	than	that	this
45	they	then	these	those	there
50	the	them	than	that	this
55	they	then	these	those	there
60					

"wh" Words Fluency Sheet

0	what	wham	whip	when	whack
5	whiz	which	why	whiff	whisk
10	what	wham	whip	when	whack
15	whiz	which	why	whiff	whisk
20	what	wham	whip	when	whack
25	whiz	which	why	whiff	whisk
30	what	wham	whip	when	whack
35	whiz	which	why	whiff	whisk
40	what	wham	whip	when	whack
45	whiz	which	why	whiff	whisk
50	what	wham	whip	when	whack
55	whiz	which	why	whiff	whisk
60					

"wh" Words Fluency Sheet

0	when	what	whale	whip	why
5	where	wheel	white	which	when
10	whack	whiz	wham	whine	wheat
15	when	what	whale	whip	why
20	where	wheel	white	which	when
25	whack	whiz	wham	whine	wheat
30	when	what	whale	whip	why
35	where	wheel	white	which	when
40	whack	whiz	wham	whine	wheat
45	when	what	whale	whip	why
50	where	wheel	white	which	when
55	whack	whiz	wham	whine	wheat
60					

"ng" Words Fluency Sheet

0	bring	gang	long	king	bang
5	sung	ring	sling	song	hung
10	fling	bring	wrong	swing	gong
15	rang	lung	fang	wing	sting
20	bring	gang	long	king	bang
25	sung	ring	sling	song	hung
30	fling	bring	wrong	swing	gong
35	rang	lung	fang	wing	sting
40	bring	gang	long	king	bang
45	sung	ring	sling	song	hung
50	fling	bring	wrong	swing	gong
55	rang	lung	fang	wing	sting
60					

"ng" Words Fluency Sheet

0	wing	hang	sting	sang	long
5	gang	ring	hung	king	rung
10	bring	bang	wrong	fang	lung
15	stung	ding	pang	cling	swung
20	wing	hang	sting	sang	long
25	gang	ring	hung	king	rung
30	bring	bang	wrong	fang	lung
35	stung	ding	pang	cling	swung
40	wing	hang	sting	sang	long
45	gang	ring	hung	king	rung
50	bring	bang	wrong	fang	lung
55	stung	ding	pang	cling	swung
60					

"mp" Words Fluency Sheet

0	stamp	limp	damp	romp	pump
5	stomp	bump	lamp	dump	ramp
10	imp	lump	limp	stump	camp
15	stamp	limp	damp	romp	pump
20	stomp	bump	lamp	dump	ramp
25	imp	lump	limp	stump	camp
30	stamp	limp	damp	romp	pump
35	stomp	bump	lamp	dump	ramp
40	imp	lump	limp	stump	camp
45	stamp	limp	damp	romp	pump
50	stomp	bump	lamp	dump	ramp
55	imp	lump	limp	stump	camp
60					

"ck" Words Fluency Sheet

0	pick	deck	sock	sick	rock
5	quack	luck	back	tack	dock
10	tick	duck	sack	kick	neck
15	pack	lock	wick	rack	tuck
20	pick	deck	sock	sick	rock
25	quack	luck	back	tack	dock
30	tick	duck	sack	kick	neck
35	pack	lock	wick	rack	tuck
40	pick	deck	sock	sick	rock
45	quack	luck	back	tack	dock
50	tick	duck	sack	kick	neck
55	pack	lock	wick	rack	tuck
60					

"nd" Words Fluency Sheet

0	send	stand	end	sand	tend
5	band	mend	pond	land	lend
10	fond	hand	bend	find	bond
15	send	stand	end	sand	tend
20	band	mend	pond	land	lend
25	fond	hand	bend	find	bond
30	send	stand	end	sand	tend
35	band	mend	pond	land	lend
40	fond	hand	bend	find	bond
45	send	stand	end	sand	tend
50	band	mend	pond	land	lend
55	fond	hand	bend	find	bond
60					

"nt" Words Fluency Sheet

0	sent	ant	want	dent	hunt
5	mint	bunt	went	vent	tent
10	punt	lint	pant	rent	hint
15	rant	lent	tint	bent	runt
20	sent	ant	want	dent	hunt
25	mint	bunt	went	vent	tent
30	punt	lint	pant	rent	hint
35	rant	lent	tint	bent	runt
40	sent	ant	want	dent	hunt
45	mint	bunt	went	vent	tent
50	punt	lint	pant	rent	hint
55	rant	lent	tint	bent	runt
60					

"tw" Words Fluency Sheet

0	twin	twig	twist	twine	twelve
5	twirl	tweet	twang	twinkle	twitter
10	tweed	twice	twenty	twitch	twirl
15	twin	twig	twist	twine	twelve
20	twirl	tweet	twang	twinkle	twitter
25	tweed	twice	twenty	twitch	twirl
30	twin	twig	twist	twine	twelve
35	twirl	tweet	twang	twinkle	twitter
40	tweed	twice	twenty	twitch	twirl
45	twin	twig	twist	twine	twelve
50	twirl	tweet	twang	twinkle	twitter
55	tweed	twice	twenty	twitch	twirl
60					

"br" Words Fluency Sheet

0	bring	broke	brat	brush	brick
5	brass	brave	Brad	brake	branch
10	bran	brand	bride	brim	brisk
15	brook	broth	brother	brown	brook
20	bring	broke	brat	brush	brick
25	brass	brave	Brad	brake	branch
30	bran	brand	bride	brim	brisk
35	brook	broth	brother	brown	brook
40	bring	broke	brat	brush	brick
45	brass	brave	Brad	brake	branch
50	bran	brand	bride	brim	brisk
55	brook	broth	brother	brown	brook
60					

"cr" Words Fluency Sheet

0	crib	crab	crane	cross	crop
5	crash	crunch	craft	crack	cry
10	crust	crook	crumb	crick	crock
15	crib	crab	crane	cross	crop
20	crash	crunch	craft	crack	cry
25	crust	crook	crumb	crick	crock
30	crib	crab	crane	cross	crop
35	crash	crunch	craft	crack	cry
40	crust	crook	crumb	crick	crock
45	crib	crab	crane	cross	crop
50	crash	crunch	craft	crack	cry
55	crust	crook	crumb	crick	crock
60					

"dr" Words Fluency Sheet

0	drop	dress	drug	drink	drip
5	drift	drill	drove	drag	drape
10	drive	drank	drum	draft	drake
15	drop	dress	drug	drink	drip
20	drift	drill	drove	drag	drape
25	drive	drank	drum	draft	drake
30	drop	dress	drug	drink	drip
35	drift	drill	drove	drag	drape
40	drive	drank	drum	draft	drake
45	drop	dress	drug	drink	drip
50	drift	drill	drove	drag	drape
55	drive	drank	drum	draft	drake
60					

"gr" Words Fluency Sheet

0	grass	grade	grand	grin	grab
5	gray	green	grant	grape	grate
10	greet	grill	grim	grip	gruff
15	grass	grade	grand	grin	grab
20	gray	green	grant	grape	grate
25	greet	grill	grim	grip	gruff
30	grass	grade	grand	grin	grab
35	gray	green	grant	grape	grate
40	greet	grill	grim	grip	gruff
45	grass	grade	grand	grin	grab
50	gray	green	grant	grape	grate
55	greet	grill	grim	grip	gruff
60					

"fr" Words Fluency Sheet

0	fresh	frizz	fry	front	frame
5	frog	from	frying	Frank	Fred
10	friend	frill	frost	free	frisk
15	fresh	frizz	fry	front	frame
20	frog	from	frying	Frank	Fred
25	friend	frill	frost	free	frisk
30	fresh	frizz	fry	front	frame
35	frog	from	frying	Frank	Fred
40	friend	frill	frost	free	frisk
45	fresh	frizz	fry	front	frame
50	frog	from	frying	Frank	Fred
55	friend	frill	frost	free	frisk
60					

"pr" Words Fluency Sheet

0	pretty	prod	prop	prize	print
5	pray	press	proud	pry	press
10	proof	prince	price	pride	probe
15	prance	present	prayer	program	prowl
20	pretty	prod	prop	prize	print
25	pray	press	proud	pry	press
30	proof	prince	price	pride	probe
35	prance	present	prayer	program	prowl
40	pretty	prod	prop	prize	print
45	pray	press	proud	pry	press
50	proof	prince	price	pride	probe
55	prance	present	prayer	program	prowl
60					

"tr" Words Fluency Sheet

0	trot	trip	tree	track	trash
5	try	truck	trek	tribe	trade
10	tramp	trap	trick	trim	trust
15	trot	trip	tree	track	trash
20	try	truck	trek	tribe	trade
25	tramp	trap	trick	trim	trust
30	trot	trip	tree	track	trash
35	try	truck	trek	tribe	trade
40	tramp	trap	trick	trim	trust
45	trot	trip	tree	track	trash
50	try	truck	trek	tribe	trade
55	tramp	trap	trick	trim	trust
60					

"bl" Words Fluency Sheet

0	black	blast	blot	bleed	blush
5	blab	blue	blink	blip	bloom
10	blend	blank	blow	blaze	blind
15	blame	blade	bless	block	bluff
20	black	blast	blot	bleed	blush
25	blab	blue	blink	blip	bloom
30	blend	blank	blow	blaze	blind
35	blame	blade	bless	block	bluff
40	black	blast	blot	bleed	blush
45	blab	blue	blink	blip	bloom
50	blend	blank	blow	blaze	blind
55	blame	blade	bless	block	bluff
60					

"cl" Words Fluency Sheet

0	cliff	clap	clam	cluck	club
5	clack	cloth	clump	clang	class
10	click	clash	clock	clamp	cling
15	clink	clip	clan	clad	clink
20	cliff	clap	clam	cluck	club
25	clack	cloth	clump	clang	class
30	click	clash	clock	clamp	cling
35	clink	clip	clan	clad	clink
40	cliff	clap	clam	cluck	club
45	clack	cloth	clump	clang	class
50	click	clash	clock	clamp	cling
55	clink	clip	clan	clad	clink
60					

"fl" Words Fluency Sheet

0	flag	flat	flap	flash	flute
5	flick	fling	fly	flame	flake
10	flesh	flush	flip	flock	flop
15	flag	flat	flap	flash	flute
20	flick	fling	fly	flame	flake
25	flesh	flush	flip	flock	flop
30	flag	flat	flap	flash	flute
35	flick	fling	fly	flame	flake
40	flesh	flush	flip	flock	flop
45	flag	flat	flap	flash	flute
50	flick	fling	fly	flame	flake
55	flesh	flush	flip	flock	flop
60					

"gl" Words Fluency Sheet

0	glad	glass	glob	glee	glide
5	globe	gloss	glum	glaze	glade
10	glad	glass	glob	glee	glide
15	globe	gloss	glum	glaze	glade
20	glad	glass	glob	glee	glide
25	globe	gloss	glum	glaze	glade
30	glad	glass	glob	glee	glide
35	globe	gloss	glum	glaze	glade
40	glad	glass	glob	glee	glide
45	globe	gloss	glum	glaze	glade
50	glad	glass	glob	glee	glide
55	globe	gloss	glum	glaze	glade
60					

"pl" Words Fluency Sheet

0	plan	plant	plot	plum	plane
5	plank	play	plod	plus	plug
10	place	player	place	plants	plums
15	plan	plant	plot	plum	plane
20	plank	play	plod	plus	plug
25	place	player	place	plants	plums
30	plan	plant	plot	plum	plane
35	plank	play	plod	plus	plug
40	place	player	place	plants	plums
45	plan	plant	plot	plum	plane
50	plank	play	plod	plus	plug
55	place	player	place	plants	plums
60					

"sc" Words Fluency Sheet

0	scab	scoot	scat	scan	scar
5	scold	scuff	scout	scoop	scoot
10	scab	scold	score	scope	scalp
15	scamp	scarf	scald	scope	scare
20	scab	scoot	scat	scan	scar
25	scold	scuff	scout	scoop	scoot
30	scab	scold	score	scope	scalp
35	scamp	scarf	scald	scope	scare
40	scab	scoot	scat	scan	scar
45	scold	scuff	scout	scoop	scoot
50	scab	scold	score	scope	scalp
55	scamp	scarf	scald	scope	scare
60					

"sm" Words Fluency Sheet

0	smack	smell	small	smash	smoke
5	smog	smock	smear	smile	smart
10	smock	smug	smith	smoky	smooth
15	smack	smell	small	smash	smoke
20	smog	smock	smear	smile	smart
25	smock	smug	smith	smoky	smooth
30	smack	smell	small	smash	smoke
35	smog	smock	smear	smile	smart
40	smock	smug	smith	smoky	smooth
45	smack	smell	small	smash	smoke
50	smog	smock	smear	smile	smart
55	smock	smug	smith	smoky	smooth
60					

"sl" Words Fluency Sheet

0	slip	slot	sled	slap	slip
5	slave	slam	slope	slept	slat
10	slash	slim	slum	slant	slate
15	slip	slot	sled	slap	slip
20	slave	slam	slope	slept	slat
25	slash	slim	slum	slant	slate
30	slip	slot	sled	slap	slip
35	slave	slam	slope	slept	slat
40	slash	slim	slum	slant	slate
45	slip	slot	sled	slap	slip
50	slave	slam	slope	slept	slat
55	slash	slim	slum	slant	slate
60					

"sk" Words Fluency Sheet

0	skunk	skin	skip	skill	sky
5	skid	skull	desk	ask	dusk
10	task	skim	mask	husk	cask
15	risk	skips	skit	musk	disk
20	skunk	skin	skip	skill	sky
25	skid	skull	desk	ask	dusk
30	task	skim	mask	husk	cask
35	risk	skips	skit	musk	disk
40	skunk	skin	skip	skill	sky
45	skid	skull	desk	ask	dusk
55	task	skim	mask	husk	cask
60					

"sn" Words Fluency Sheet

0	sniff	snore	snug	snack	snatch
5	snob	snub	snap	snip	snare
10	snag	snake	sneeze	snuff	snoop
15	sniff	snore	snug	snack	snatch
20	snob	snub	snap	snip	snare
25	snag	snake	sneeze	snuff	snoop
30	sniff	snore	snug	snack	snatch
35	snob	snub	snap	snip	snare
40	snag	snake	sneeze	snuff	snoop
45	sniff	snore	snug	snack	snatch
50	snob	snub	snap	snip	snare
55	snag	snake	sneeze	snuff	snoop
60					

"sp" Words Fluency Sheet

0	span	spell	sped	spy	spend
5	speck	spill	spin	spot	spoke
10	spent	spike	spine	speed	spun
15	span	spell	sped	spy	spend
20	speck	spill	spin	spot	spoke
25	spent	spike	spine	speed	spun
30	span	spell	sped	spy	spend
35	speck	spill	spin	spot	spoke
40	spent	spike	spine	speed	spun
45	span	spell	sped	spy	spend
50	speck	spill	spin	spot	spoke
55	spent	spike	spine	speed	spun
60					

"st" Words Fluency Sheet

0	stop	nest	step	just	still
5	fast	dust	west	pest	last
10	past	best	lost	stand	stall
15	rust	rest	stack	stem	cast
20	stop	nest	step	just	still
25	fast	dust	west	pest	last
30	past	best	lost	stand	stall
35	rust	rest	stack	stem	cast
40	stop	nest	step	just	still
45	fast	dust	west	pest	last
50	past	best	lost	stand	stall
55	rust	rest	stack	stem	cast
60					

"sw" Words Fluency Sheet

0	swap	swan	swat	swam	swell
5	swim	swift	swept	swoop	swing
10	sway	sweet	swish	swamp	swarm
15	sweat	swine	sweep	swatch	sworn
20	swap	swan	swat	swam	swell
25	swim	swift	swept	swoop	swing
30	sway	sweet	swish	swamp	swarm
35	sweat	swine	sweep	swatch	sworn
40	swap	swan	swat	swam	swell
45	swim	swift	swept	swoop	swing
50	sway	sweet	swish	swamp	swarm
55	sweat	swine	sweep	swatch	sworn
60					

Long "a" Words Fluency Sheet

0	fade	take	cake	tale	came
5	name	made	sake	game	cane
10	lake	gave	tame	maze	make
15	gate	case	late	lame	base
20	fade	take	cake	tale	came
25	name	made	sake	game	cane
30	lake	gave	tame	maze	make
35	gate	case	late	lame	base
40	fade	take	cake	tale	came
45	name	made	sake	game	cane
50	lake	gave	tame	maze	make
55	gate	case	late	lame	base
60					

Long "a" Words Fluency Sheet

0	rake	wade	bake	cape	name
5	vase	sale	gate	cave	late
10	gave	gaze	gate	tape	cake
15	cane	page	made	race	cage
20	rake	wade	bake	cape	name
25	vase	sale	gate	cave	late
30	gave	gaze	gate	tape	cake
35	cane	page	made	race	cage
40	rake	wade	bake	cape	name
45	vase	sale	gate	cave	late
50	gave	gaze	gate	tape	cake
55	cane	page	made	race	cage
60					

Discrimination Practice

0	tag	fade	glad	take	cake
5	tale	stab	came	sag	name
10	trap	made	cab	sake	game
15	cane	task	lake	pack	gave
20	bat	tame	can	maze	make
25	gate	flat	case	blab	late
30	camp	lame	ran	base	fade
35	rake	cat	wade	ram	sat
40	brag	bake	slam	cape	brat
45	name	clap	vase	sat	man
50	pad	sale	dad	gate	drag
55	tape	flag	cake	rat	hat
60					

Long "i" Words Fluency Sheet

0	rice	life	mice	ride	hike
5	mile	fine	pipe	nine	wise
10	kite	five	fire	line	fire
15	vine	bike	pile	nice	side
20	rice	life	mice	ride	hike
25	mile	fine	pipe	nine	wise
30	kite	five	fire	line	fire
35	vine	bike	pile	nice	side
40	rice	life	mice	ride	hike
45	mile	fine	pipe	nine	wise
50	kite	five	fire	line	fire
55	vine	bike	pile	nice	side
60					

Long "i" Words Fluency Sheet

0	hide	rice	like	nine	pipe
5	dime	mile	ride	bike	ice
10	mine	hike	ripe	side	wise
15	nice	line	pine	lime	mile
20	hide	rice	like	nine	pipe
25	dime	mile	ride	bike	ice
30	mine	hike	ripe	side	wise
35	nice	line	pine	lime	mile
40	hide	rice	like	nine	pipe
45	dime	mile	ride	bike	ice
50	mine	hike	ripe	side	wise
55	nice	line	pine	lime	mile
60					

Discrimination Practice

0	rice	mint	fig	vine	kit
5	fib	life	hide	milk	bid
10	like	sing	mice	pin	rid
15	silk	bike	gift	ride	bit
20	nine	lid	pile	list	hike
25	dim	pipe	sink	fin	mile
30	nice	mist	sit	fine	pit
35	king	rig	pipe	him	dime
40	six	nine	risk	zip	fit
45	wise	pick	win	side	lime
50	big	kite	fist	mile	pit
55	hip	rib	five	did	sit
60					

Long "e" Words Fluency Sheet

0	meet	heat	tree	seal	beak
5	beat	dear	feed	feet	seat
10	bean	near	see	need	heal
15	keep	read	mean	peek	seen
20	meet	heat	tree	seal	beak
25	beat	dear	feed	feet	seat
30	bean	near	see	need	heal
35	keep	read	mean	peek	seen
40	meet	heat	tree	seal	beak
45	beat	dear	feed	feet	seat
50	bean	near	see	need	heal
55	keep	read	mean	peek	seen
60					

Long "e" Words Fluency Sheet

0	bee	deep	bean	sea	beak
5	leap	east	seal	neat	heap
10	heel	meal	leak	mean	free
15	feed	seen	feet	heat	bead
20	bee	deep	bean	sea	beak
25	leap	east	seal	neat	heap
30	heel	meal	leak	mean	free
35	feed	seen	feet	heat	bead
40	bee	deep	bean	sea	beak
45	leap	east	seal	neat	heap
50	heel	meal	leak	mean	free
55	feed	seen	feet	heat	bead
60					

Discrimination Practice

0	meet	deck	deep	met	red
5	yes	heat	rest	leap	leg
10	self	led	tree	hem	get
15	pep	east	left	seal	pep
20	neat	send	wed	pen	beak
25	let	beat	help	heap	leg
30	heel	pet	dear	bed	next
35	belt	meal	hen	feed	beg
40	set	wept	leak	web	feet
45	mean	den	seat	met	dent
50	bed	nest	web	bean	ten
55	went	free	yet	red	need
60					

Long "o" Words Fluency Sheet

0	joke	rode	hope	note	home
5	bone	code	rope	rose	woke
10	vote	doze	poke	hole	lone
15	robe	nose	mole	hose	cone
20	joke	rode	hope	note	home
25	bone	code	rope	rose	woke
30	vote	doze	poke	hole	lone
35	robe	nose	mole	hose	cone
40	joke	rode	hope	note	home
45	bone	code	rope	rose	woke
50	vote	doze	poke	hole	lone
55	robe	nose	mole	hose	cone
60					

Long "o" Words Fluency Sheet

0	robe	joke	hole	code	home
5	rope	vote	wove	woke	pole
10	rode	mole	poke	bone	nose
15	lone	note	zone	woke	Rome
20	robe	joke	hole	code	home
25	rope	vote	wove	woke	pole
30	rode	mole	poke	bone	nose
35	lone	note	zone	woke	Rome
40	robe	joke	hole	code	home
45	rope	vote	wove	woke	pole
50	rode	mole	poke	bone	nose
55	lone	note	zone	woke	Rome
60					

Discrimination Practice

0	robe	rock	bone	top	cot
5	box	joke	mock	nose	got
10	lone	mop	hole	not	sock
15	bond	note	fox	code	sod
20	sob	cop	romp	dot	home
25	zone	fond	lot	rope	tot
30	jog	rod	vote	cob	rock
35	cost	wove	pop	woke	nod
40	woke	got	poke	mob	lock
45	fox	pole	pod	lost	lop
50	rose	sod	rode	cod	spot
55	drop	doze	snob	mole	crop
60					

Long "u" Words Fluency Sheet

0	cube	use	fume	rude	cute
5	dude	June	mute	tune	fuse
10	huge	flute	crude	mule	lute
15	cube	use	fume	rude	cute
20	dude	June	mute	tune	fuse
25	huge	flute	crude	mule	lute
30	cube	use	fume	rude	cute
35	dude	June	mute	tune	fuse
40	huge	flute	crude	mule	lute
45	cube	use	fume	rude	cute
50	dude	June	mute	tune	fuse
55	huge	flute	crude	mule	lute
60					

Long "u" Words Fluency Sheet

0	cute	use	cue	huge	cube
5	mule	fume	uses	fuse	flute
10	cute	use	cue	huge	cube
15	mule	fume	uses	fuse	flute
20	cute	use	cue	huge	cube
25	mule	fume	uses	fuse	flute
30	cute	use	cue	huge	cube
35	mule	fume	uses	fuse	flute
40	cute	use	cue	huge	cube
45	mule	fume	uses	fuse	flute
50	cute	use	cue	huge	cube
55	mule	fume	uses	fuse	flute
60					

Discrimination Practice

0	rude	slug	cute	bus	hum
5	cub	dude	club	huge	bug
10	cube	run	June	snub	cup
15	plum	mule	rug	tune	mud
20	sum	smug	fume	pop	flute
25	gum	crude	fun	fuse	stub
30	cue	bud	lute	glum	tub
35	dug	plus	rub	rude	hug
40	drum	mud	dude	nut	cube
45	use	rub	drug	cut	jug
50	sun	fume	jut	fuse	spun
55	cue	slum	mute	bun	mug
60					

"ai" Words Fluency Sheet

0	pain	laid	sail	paid	rain
5	train	snail	maid	paint	brain
10	jail	chain	raid	mail	main
15	stain	tail	bait	drain	nail
20	trail	wait	rail	plain	faint
25	pain	laid	sail	paid	rain
30	train	snail	maid	paint	brain
35	jail	chain	raid	mail	main
40	stain	tail	bait	drain	nail
45	trail	wait	rail	plain	faint
50	pain	laid	sail	paid	rain
55	train	snail	maid	paint	brain
60					

"ay" Words Fluency Sheet

0	day	play	say	may	hay
5	pay	ray	tray	stay	pray
10	sway	clay	gray	jay	bay
15	way	lay	spray	stray	slay
20	day	play	say	may	hay
25	pay	ray	tray	stay	pray
30	sway	clay	gray	jay	bay
35	way	lay	spray	stray	slay
40	day	play	say	may	hay
45	pay	ray	tray	stay	pray
50	sway	clay	gray	jay	bay
55	way	lay	spray	stray	slay
60					

"ee" Words Fluency Sheet

0	see	feed	meet	cheek	seem
5	peel	green	sheep	sheet	speed
10	need	speech	knee	deep	bleed
15	week	wheel	three	weed	peek
20	keep	seek	heel	tree	queen
25	see	feed	meet	cheek	seem
30	peel	green	sheep	sheet	speed
35	need	speech	knee	deep	bleed
40	week	wheel	three	weed	peek
45	keep	seek	heel	tree	queen
50	see	feed	meet	cheek	seem
55	peel	green	sheep	sheet	speed
60					

"ea" Words Fluency Sheet

0	eat	mean	team	steal	meal
5	sea	read	seal	teach	cream
10	speak	tea	clean	leap	dear
15	feast	near	leave	beach	leak
20	bead	beak	cheap	heat	real
25	eat	mean	team	steal	meal
30	sea	read	seal	teach	cream
35	speak	tea	clean	leap	dear
40	feast	near	leave	beach	leak
45	bead	beak	cheap	heat	real
50	eat	mean	team	steal	meal
55	sea	read	seal	teach	cream
60					

"oa" Words Fluency Sheet

0	boat	coast	float	moan	road
5	coal	toad	coach	soak	toast
10	coat	goal	load	groan	cloak
15	loan	foam	roast	croak	boast
20	boat	coast	float	moan	road
25	coal	toad	coach	soak	toast
30	coat	goal	load	groan	cloak
35	loan	foam	roast	croak	boast
40	boat	coast	float	moan	road
45	coal	toad	coach	soak	toast
50	coat	goal	load	groan	cloak
55	loan	foam	roast	croak	boast
60					

"ow" (as in *low*) Words Fluency Sheet

0	show	slow	know	crow	bow
5	mow	shown	row	blow	snow
10	low	grow	flown	tow	flow
15	known	glow	crow	grown	grow
20	show	slow	know	crow	bow
25	mow	shown	row	blow	snow
30	low	grow	flown	tow	flow
35	known	glow	crow	grown	grow
40	show	slow	know	crow	bow
45	mow	shown	row	blow	snow
50	low	grow	flown	tow	flow
55	known	glow	crow	grown	grow
60					

"ow" (as in *how*) Words Fluency Sheet

0	now	brown	plow	owl	how
5	chow	howl	clown	cow	growl
10	down	prowl	wow	fowl	gown
15	town	vow	scowl	crown	brown
20	now	brown	plow	owl	how
25	chow	howl	clown	cow	growl
30	down	prowl	wow	fowl	gown
35	town	vow	scowl	crown	brown
40	now	brown	plow	owl	how
45	chow	howl	clown	cow	growl
50	down	prowl	wow	fowl	gown
55	town	vow	scowl	crown	brown
60					

"oy" (as in *boy*) Words Fluency Sheet

0	joy	boy	coy	toy	Roy
5	Troy	soy	ploy	toys	boys
10	joy	boy	coy	toy	Roy
15	Troy	soy	ploy	toys	boys
20	joy	boy	coy	toy	Roy
25	Troy	soy	ploy	toys	boys
30	joy	boy	coy	toy	Roy
35	Troy	soy	ploy	toys	boys
40	joy	boy	coy	toy	Roy
45	Troy	soy	ploy	toys	boys
50	joy	boy	coy	toy	Roy
55	Troy	soy	ploy	toys	boys
60					

"oi" (as in *boil*) Words Fluency Sheet

0	boil	coin	coil	noise	oil
5	point	toil	spoil	join	joint
10	soil	loin	moist	foil	broil
15	boil	coin	coil	noise	oil
20	point	toil	spoil	join	joint
25	soil	loin	moist	foil	broil
30	boil	coin	coil	noise	oil
35	point	toil	spoil	join	joint
40	soil	loin	moist	foil	broil
45	boil	coin	coil	noise	oil
50	point	toil	spoil	join	joint
60					

"ou" (as in *out*) Words Fluency Sheet

0	out	count	cloud	loud	mouse
5	south	shout	hour	proud	sour
10	scout	flour	found	ouch	sound
15	mouth	grouch	mount	round	house
20	out	count	cloud	loud	mouse
25	south	shout	hour	proud	sour
30	scout	flour	found	ouch	sound
35	mouth	grouch	mount	round	house
40	out	count	cloud	loud	mouse
45	south	shout	hour	proud	sour
50	scout	flour	found	ouch	sound
55	mouth	grouch	mount	round	house
60					

"aw" (as in *saw*) Words Fluency Sheet

0	law	fawn	saw	crawl	jaw
5	lawn	draw	yawn	caw	bawl
10	paw	drawn	claw	dawn	raw
15	brawn	slaw	straw	shawl	raw
20	law	fawn	saw	crawl	jaw
25	lawn	draw	yawn	caw	bawl
30	paw	drawn	claw	dawn	raw
35	brawn	slaw	straw	shawl	raw
40	law	fawn	saw	crawl	jaw
45	lawn	draw	yawn	caw	bawl
50	paw	drawn	claw	dawn	raw
55	brawn	slaw	straw	shawl	raw
60					

"oo" (as in *moon*) Words Fluency Sheet

0	fool	moon	hoop	cool	shoot
5	moo	goose	food	too	spoon
10	tooth	soon	loot	school	roof
15	hoot	loop	boo	coop	room
20	fool	moon	hoop	cool	shoot
25	moo	goose	food	too	spoon
30	tooth	soon	loot	school	roof
35	hoot	loop	boo	coop	room
40	fool	moon	hoop	cool	shoot
45	moo	goose	food	too	spoon
50	tooth	soon	loot	school	roof
55	hoot	loop	boo	coop	room
60					

"oo" (as in *book*) Words Fluency Sheet

0	book	good	shook	foot	woof
5	hook	crook	cook	stood	brook
10	hood	wood	look	hook	wool
15	nook	hoof	soot	took	books
20	book	good	shook	foot	woof
25	hook	crook	cook	stood	brook
30	hood	wood	look	hook	wool
35	nook	hoof	soot	took	books
40	book	good	shook	foot	woof
45	hook	crook	cook	stood	brook
50	hood	wood	look	hook	wool
55	nook	hoof	soot	took	books
60					

"igh" Vowel-Pattern Fluency Sheet

0	high	right	sigh	tight	night
5	sight	light	might	flight	bright
10	right	fright	thigh	fight	knight
15	high	right	sigh	tight	night
20	sight	light	might	flight	bright
25	right	fright	thigh	fight	knight
30	high	right	sigh	tight	night
35	sight	light	might	flight	bright
40	right	fright	thigh	fight	knight
45	high	right	sigh	tight	night
50	sight	light	might	flight	bright
55	right	fright	thigh	fight	knight
60					

"y" Vowel-Pattern Fluency Sheet

0	shy	why	by	cry	fly
5	try	dry	fry	spy	my
10	pry	shy	spry	sly	guy
15	shy	why	by	cry	fly
20	try	dry	fry	spy	my
25	pry	shy	spry	sly	guy
30	shy	why	by	cry	fly
35	try	dry	fry	spy	my
40	pry	shy	spry	sly	guy
45	shy	why	by	cry	fly
50	try	dry	fry	spy	my
55	pry	shy	spry	sly	guy
60					

"ar" Words Fluency Sheet

0	card	far	jar	arm	harp
5	bark	yard	car	part	shark
10	hard	sharp	smart	dark	barn
15	farm	star	park	scar	yarn
20	chart	cart	tar	start	mark
25	card	far	jar	arm	harp
30	bark	yard	car	part	shark
35	hard	sharp	smart	dark	barn
40	farm	star	park	scar	yarn
45	chart	cart	tar	start	mark
50	card	far	jar	arm	harp
55	bark	yard	car	part	shark
60					

"ar" Words Fluency Sheet

0	far	card	park	star	farm
5	cart	barn	yard	jar	harp
10	arm	tar	part	hard	harm
15	dart	yarn	scar	car	sharp
20	far	card	park	star	farm
25	cart	barn	yard	jar	harp
30	arm	tar	part	hard	harm
35	dart	yarn	scar	car	sharp
40	far	card	park	star	farm
45	cart	barn	yard	jar	harp
50	arm	tar	part	hard	harm
55	dart	yarn	scar	car	sharp
60					

"er" Words Fluency Sheet

0	fern	jerk	germ	verb	stern
5	term	clerk	herb	perk	intern
10	fern	jerk	germ	verb	stern
15	term	clerk	herb	perk	intern
20	fern	jerk	germ	verb	stern
25	term	clerk	herb	perk	intern
30	fern	jerk	germ	verb	stern
35	term	clerk	herb	perk	intern
40	fern	jerk	germ	verb	stern
45	term	clerk	herb	perk	intern
50	fern	jerk	germ	verb	stern
55	term	clerk	herb	perk	intern
60					

"er" Words Fluency Sheet

0	verb	her	fern	term	clerk
5	serve	jerk	germ	nerve	stern
10	verb	her	fern	term	clerk
15	serve	jerk	germ	nerve	stern
20	verb	her	fern	term	clerk
25	serve	jerk	germ	nerve	stern
30	verb	her	fern	term	clerk
35	serve	jerk	germ	nerve	stern
40	verb	her	fern	term	clerk
45	serve	jerk	germ	nerve	stern
50	verb	her	fern	term	clerk
55	serve	jerk	germ	nerve	stern
60					

"or" Words Fluency Sheet

0	fork	cord	door	for	sort
5	more	torn	born	short	floor
10	corn	pork	porch	store	thorn
15	snore	lord	storm	sport	horn
20	fork	cord	door	for	sort
25	more	torn	born	short	floor
30	corn	pork	porch	store	thorn
35	snore	lord	storm	sport	horn
40	fork	cord	door	for	sort
45	more	torn	born	short	floor
50	corn	pork	porch	store	thorn
55	snore	lord	storm	sport	horn
60					

"or" Words Fluency Sheet

0	port	torn	fork	sore	form
5	pork	torch	lord	sort	cork
10	porch	storm	cord	more	born
15	store	fort	horn	short	torn
20	port	torn	fork	sore	form
25	pork	torch	lord	sort	cork
30	porch	storm	cord	more	born
35	store	fort	horn	short	torn
40	port	torn	fork	sore	form
45	pork	torch	lord	sort	cork
50	porch	storm	cord	more	born
55	store	fort	horn	short	torn
60					

"ir" Words Fluency Sheet

0	stir	bird	dirt	first	birth
5	shirt	sir	girl	skirt	fir
10	whirl	third	thirst	flirt	whir
15	shirk	twirl	mirth	swirl	squirt
20	stir	bird	dirt	first	birth
25	shirt	sir	girl	skirt	fir
30	whirl	third	thirst	flirt	whir
35	shirk	twirl	mirth	swirl	squirt
40	stir	bird	dirt	first	birth
45	shirt	sir	girl	skirt	fir
50	whirl	third	thirst	flirt	whir
55	shirk	twirl	mirth	swirl	squirt
60					

"ir" Words Fluency Sheet

0	dirt	first	girl	bird	stir
5	stir	shirt	thirst	twirl	third
10	birth	whirl	sir	skirt	squirt
15	dirt	first	girl	bird	stir
20	stir	shirt	thirst	twirl	third
25	birth	whirl	sir	skirt	squirt
30	dirt	first	girl	bird	stir
35	stir	shirt	thirst	twirl	third
40	birth	whirl	sir	skirt	squirt
45	dirt	first	girl	bird	stir
50	stir	shirt	thirst	twirl	third
55	birth	whirl	sir	skirt	squirt
60					

"ur" Words Fluency Sheet

0	turn	fur	curb	nurse	hurt
5	blur	curl	purse	spurt	churn
10	burn	lurk	urge	spur	blurt
15	turn	fur	curb	nurse	hurt
20	blur	curl	purse	spurt	churn
25	burn	lurk	urge	spur	blurt
30	turn	fur	curb	nurse	hurt
35	blur	curl	purse	spurt	churn
40	burn	lurk	urge	spur	blurt
45	turn	fur	curb	nurse	hurt
50	blur	curl	purse	spurt	churn
55	burn	lurk	urge	spur	blurt
60					

"ur" Words Fluency Sheet

0	curl	fur	curb	burn	lurk
5	turn	spur	hurl	blurb	churn
10	hurt	nurse	urge	urn	blur
15	murk	spurt	spurn	purse	blurt
20	curl	fur	curb	burn	lurk
25	turn	spur	hurl	blurb	churn
30	hurt	nurse	urge	urn	blur
35	murk	spurt	spurn	purse	blurt
40	curl	fur	curb	burn	lurk
45	turn	spur	hurl	blurb	churn
50	hurt	nurse	urge	urn	blur
55	murk	spurt	spurn	purse	blurt
60					

List 1

| 0 | the | of | and | to | a |
| 5 | in | that | is | was | he |

| 10 | the | of | and | to | a |
| 15 | in | that | is | was | he |

| 20 | the | of | and | to | a |
| 25 | in | that | is | was | he |

| 30 | the | of | and | to | a |
| 35 | in | that | is | was | he |

| 40 | the | of | and | to | a |
| 45 | in | that | is | was | he |

| 50 | the | of | and | to | a |
| 55 | in | that | is | was | he |

| 60 | | | | | |

List 2

0	for	it	with	as	his
5	on	be	at	by	I
10	for	it	with	as	his
15	on	be	at	by	I
20	for	it	with	as	his
25	on	be	at	by	I
30	for	it	with	as	his
35	on	be	at	by	I
40	for	it	with	as	his
45	on	be	at	by	I
50	for	it	with	as	his
55	on	be	at	by	I
60					

List 3

0	this	had	not	are	but
5	from	or	have	an	they
10	this	had	not	are	but
15	from	or	have	an	they
20	this	had	not	are	but
25	from	or	have	an	they
30	this	had	not	are	but
35	from	or	have	an	they
40	this	had	not	are	but
45	from	or	have	an	they
50	this	had	not	are	but
55	from	or	have	an	they
60					

List 4

0	which	one	you	were	her
5	all	she	there	would	their
10	which	one	you	were	her
15	all	she	there	would	their
20	which	one	you	were	her
25	all	she	there	would	their
30	which	one	you	were	her
35	all	she	there	would	their
40	which	one	you	were	her
45	all	she	there	would	their
50	which	one	you	were	her
55	all	she	there	would	their
60					

List 5

0	we	him	been	has	when
5	who	will	more	no	if
10	we	him	been	has	when
15	who	will	more	no	if
20	we	him	been	has	when
25	who	will	more	no	if
30	we	him	been	has	when
35	who	will	more	no	if
40	we	him	been	has	when
45	who	will	more	no	if
50	we	him	been	has	when
55	who	will	more	no	if
60					

List 6

0	out	so	said	what	up
5	its	about	into	than	them
10	out	so	said	what	up
15	its	about	into	than	them
20	out	so	said	what	up
25	its	about	into	than	them
30	out	so	said	what	up
35	its	about	into	than	them
40	out	so	said	what	up
45	its	about	into	than	them
50	out	so	said	what	up
55	its	about	into	than	them
60					

List 7

0	can	only	other	new	some
5	time	could	these	two	may
10	can	only	other	new	some
15	time	could	these	two	may
20	can	only	other	new	some
25	time	could	these	two	may
30	can	only	other	new	some
35	time	could	these	two	may
40	can	only	other	new	some
45	time	could	these	two	may
50	can	only	other	new	some
55	time	could	these	two	may
60					

List 8

0	then	do	first	any	my
5	now	such	like	our	over
10	then	do	first	any	my
15	now	such	like	our	over
20	then	do	first	any	my
25	now	such	like	our	over
30	then	do	first	any	my
35	now	such	like	our	over
40	then	do	first	any	my
45	now	such	like	our	over
50	then	do	first	any	my
55	now	such	like	our	over
60					

List 9

0	man	me	even	most	made
5	after	also	did	many	before
10	man	me	even	most	made
15	after	also	did	many	before
20	man	me	even	most	made
25	after	also	did	many	before
30	man	me	even	most	made
35	after	also	did	many	before
40	man	me	even	most	made
45	after	also	did	many	before
50	man	me	even	most	made
55	after	also	did	many	before
60					

List 10

0	must	through	back	years	where
5	much	your	way	well	down
10	must	through	back	years	where
15	much	your	way	well	down
20	must	through	back	years	where
25	much	your	way	well	down
30	must	through	back	years	where
35	much	your	way	well	down
40	must	through	back	years	where
45	much	your	way	well	down
50	must	through	back	years	where
55	much	your	way	well	down
60					

List 11

0	should	because	each	just	those
5	people	Mr.	how	too	little
10	should	because	each	just	those
15	people	Mr.	how	too	little
20	should	because	each	just	those
25	people	Mr.	how	too	little
30	should	because	each	just	those
35	people	Mr.	how	too	little
40	should	because	each	just	those
45	people	Mr.	how	too	little
50	should	because	each	just	those
55	people	Mr.	how	too	little
60					

List 12

0	us	state	good	very	make
5	world	still	see	own	men
10	us	state	good	very	make
15	world	still	see	own	men
20	us	state	good	very	make
25	world	still	see	own	men
30	us	state	good	very	make
35	world	still	see	own	men
40	us	state	good	very	make
45	world	still	see	own	men
50	us	state	good	very	make
55	world	still	see	own	men
60					

List 13

0	work	long	here	get	both
5	between	life	being	under	never
10	work	long	here	get	both
15	between	life	being	under	never
20	work	long	here	get	both
25	between	life	being	under	never
30	work	long	here	get	both
35	between	life	being	under	never
40	work	long	here	get	both
45	between	life	being	under	never
50	work	long	here	get	both
55	between	life	being	under	never
60					

List 14

0	day	same	another	know	year
5	while	last	might	great	old
10	day	same	another	know	year
15	while	last	might	great	old
20	day	same	another	know	year
25	while	last	might	great	old
30	day	same	another	know	year
35	while	last	might	great	old
40	day	same	another	know	year
45	while	last	might	great	old
50	day	same	another	know	year
55	while	last	might	great	old
60					

List 15

0	off	come	since	go	against
5	came	right	states	used	take
10	off	come	since	go	against
15	came	right	states	used	take
20	off	come	since	go	against
25	came	right	states	used	take
30	off	come	since	go	against
35	came	right	states	used	take
40	off	come	since	go	against
45	came	right	states	used	take
50	off	come	since	go	against
55	came	right	states	used	take
60					

List 16

0	three	himself	few	house	use
5	during	without	again	place	American
10	three	himself	few	house	use
15	during	without	again	place	American
20	three	himself	few	house	use
25	during	without	again	place	American
30	three	himself	few	house	use
35	during	without	again	place	American
40	three	himself	few	house	use
45	during	without	again	place	American
50	three	himself	few	house	use
55	during	without	again	place	American
60					

List 17

0	around	however	home	small	found
5	Mrs.	thought	went	say	part
10	around	however	home	small	found
15	Mrs.	thought	went	say	part
20	around	however	home	small	found
25	Mrs.	thought	went	say	part
30	around	however	home	small	found
35	Mrs.	thought	went	say	part
40	around	however	home	small	found
45	Mrs.	thought	went	say	part
50	around	however	home	small	found
55	Mrs.	thought	went	say	part
60					

List 18

0	once	high	general	upon	school
5	every	don't	does	got	united
10	once	high	general	upon	school
15	every	don't	does	got	united
20	once	high	general	upon	school
25	every	don't	does	got	united
30	once	high	general	upon	school
35	every	don't	does	got	united
40	once	high	general	upon	school
45	every	don't	does	got	united
50	once	high	general	upon	school
55	every	don't	does	got	united
60					

List 19

0	left	number	course	war	until
5	always	away	something	fact	water
10	left	number	course	war	until
15	always	away	something	fact	water
20	left	number	course	war	until
25	always	away	something	fact	water
30	left	number	course	war	until
35	always	away	something	fact	water
40	left	number	course	war	until
45	always	away	something	fact	water
50	left	number	course	war	until
55	always	away	something	fact	water
60					

List 20

0	though	less	public	put	think
5	almost	hand	enough	far	look
10	though	less	public	put	think
15	almost	hand	enough	far	look
20	though	less	public	put	think
25	almost	hand	enough	far	look
30	though	less	public	put	think
35	almost	hand	enough	far	look
40	though	less	public	put	think
45	almost	hand	enough	far	look
50	though	less	public	put	think
55	almost	hand	enough	far	look
60					

List 21

0	head	yet	government	system	set
5	better	told	nothing	night	end
10	head	yet	government	system	set
15	better	told	nothing	night	end
20	head	yet	government	system	set
25	better	told	nothing	night	end
30	head	yet	government	system	set
35	better	told	nothing	night	end
40	head	yet	government	system	set
45	better	told	nothing	night	end
50	head	yet	government	system	set
55	better	told	nothing	night	end
60					

List 22

0	why	didn't	know	eyes	find
5	going	look	asked	later	point
10	why	didn't	know	eyes	find
15	going	look	asked	later	point
20	why	didn't	know	eyes	find
25	going	look	asked	later	point
30	why	didn't	know	eyes	find
35	going	look	asked	later	point
40	why	didn't	know	eyes	find
45	going	look	asked	later	point
50	why	didn't	know	eyes	find
55	going	look	asked	later	point
60					

List 23

0	knew	city	next	program	business
5	give	group	toward	days	young
10	knew	city	next	program	business
15	give	group	toward	days	young
20	knew	city	next	program	business
25	give	group	toward	days	young
30	knew	city	next	program	business
35	give	group	toward	days	young
40	knew	city	next	program	business
45	give	group	toward	days	young
50	knew	city	next	program	business
55	give	group	toward	days	young
60					

List 24

0	let	room	president	side	social
5	present	given	several	order	national
10	let	room	president	side	social
15	present	given	several	order	national
20	let	room	president	side	social
25	present	given	several	order	national
30	let	room	president	side	social
35	present	given	several	order	national
40	let	room	president	side	social
45	present	given	several	order	national
50	let	room	president	side	social
55	present	given	several	order	national
60					

List 25

0	second	possible	rather	per	face
5	among	form	important	often	things
10	second	possible	rather	per	face
15	among	form	important	often	things
20	second	possible	rather	per	face
25	among	form	important	often	things
30	second	possible	rather	per	face
35	among	form	important	often	things
40	second	possible	rather	per	face
45	among	form	important	often	things
50	second	possible	rather	per	face
55	among	form	important	often	things
60					

Decodable Short-Vowel and Long-Vowel Stories

These 20 decodable stories may be used as review or extension activities to reinforce targeted phonetic elements in a teacher-led, small-group setting. Instructional options include:

- Teacher and students choral-read the story together.
- Teacher reads each sentence aloud, and students "echo" read the sentence.
- Teacher reads the story aloud as students follow along and fill in any words that the teacher intentionally leaves out.
- Student partnerships or small groups take turns reading alternate sentences of the story.
- Students individually whisper-read the story as the teacher monitors.

As students master the phonetic elements, they may take the decodable stories home for additional reading practice.

Decodable Short-Vowel Stories
(in order of phonetic element introduction)

Short "a" stories:
  Hats and Caps
  Matt and His Cats

Short "i" stories:
  Kim Is Six
  Kit the Pig

Short "e" stories:
  Bess the Hen
  Meg and the Wet Pet

Short "o" stories:
  Dot's Job
  Bob the Frog

Short "u" stories:
  Mutt the Pup
  Bud the Bug

Decodable Long-Vowel Stories
(in order of phonetic element introduction)

Long "a" stories:
  Dave and Jake
  Kate's Big Cake

Long "i" stories:
  Mike at Camp
  Cakes and Pies

Long "e" stories:
  The Team
  The Mean Queen

Long "o" stories:
  Joe the Mole
  Rose Rode Horses

Long "u" stories:
  Luke the Mule
  The Duke's Mule

Short "a" Story: Hats and Caps

Decodable Words	Automatic Words	
and	who	with
Pat	like	red
Pam	likes	blue
Sam	they	have
Dan	many	
pals	all	
hats	the	
caps	fun	

Hats and Caps

0   Pat and Pam are pals who like hats. Pat likes red hats,

12   and Pam likes blue hats. They have many hats.

21   Sam and Dan are pals who like caps. Sam likes red

32   caps, and Dan likes blue caps. They have many caps.

42   All the pals have fun with hats and caps.

51

Total Words Read _____

– Errors _____

= CWPM _____

Short "a" Story: Matt and His Cats

Decodable Words		Automatic Words	
Matt	jam	who	on
man	pan	likes	
cats	nap	are	
Nan	lap	the	
Sam		his	
tan		they	
fat		played	
cats		by	
tag		then	
ran		them	
ham		took	

Matt and His Cats

0   Matt is a man who likes cats. Nan and Sam are his

12   tan, fat cats.

15   The cats played tag. Nan and Sam ran and ran. They

26   ran by a cab and a van. Then Matt got them ham and jam

40   in a pan. The cats took a nap on Matt's lap.

51

Total Words Read _____

− Errors _____

= CWPM _____

           Decodable Short-Vowel and Long-Vowel Stories   **261**

Short "i" Story: Kim Is Six

Decodable Words		Automatic Words
Kim	pigs	is
six	wigs	she
and		likes
has		car
kits		also
big		red
pins		
tin		
lids		
pink		

Kim Is Six

0   Kim is six, and she likes six! Kim has six car kits and

13   six big pins. She also has six tin lids. Kim has six pink pigs

27   and six red wigs.

31   Six car kits, six big pins, six tin lids, six pink pigs, and

44   six red wigs! Kim likes six!

50

Total Words Read _____

− Errors _____

= CWPM _____

Short "i" Story: Kit the Pig

Decodable Words	Automatic Words
Kit	the
pig	is
big	a
pink	likes
dig	to
sit	he
swim	and
Skip	too

Kit the Pig

0   Kit is a pig. Kit is a big, pink pig. Kit likes to dig. He

15 likes to sit and dig. Kit likes to swim. He likes to dig and

29 swim.

30   Skip is a big pink pig, too. He likes to dig and swim.

43 Kit and Skip like to dig and swim.

51

Total Words Read _____

− Errors _____

= CWPM _____

Short "e" Story: Bess the Hen

Decodable Words	Automatic Words
Bess	is
hen	a
red	she
yes	lives
big	then
pen	chicks
had	the
nest	her
ten	
eggs	

Bess the Hen

0   Bess is a hen. She is a red hen. Yes, Bess is a big, red

15   hen. Bess lives in a pen. She had a nest in the pen. Bess

29   had a big nest in the pen.

36   Bess had ten eggs in her nest. Then Bess had ten

47   chicks in her nest.

51

Total Words Read _____

– Errors _____

= CWPM _____

Short "e" Story: Meg and the Wet Pet

Decodable Words		Automatic Words
Meg	mad	a
had	sent	the
pet	bed	was
cat		got
Ben		were
sat		to
wet		they
sand		too
mess		
dad		

Meg and the Wet Pet

0   Meg had a pet cat. The cat was Ben. Meg and Ben sat

13   in the wet sand. They got wet. Meg and Ben were a wet

26   mess.

27   Dad was mad that they were a mess. Meg was sent to

39   bed. Ben was sent to bed, too. Meg and her pet went to

52   bed. They were sad.

56

Total Words Read _____

– Errors _____

= CWPM _____

Short "o" Story: Dot's Job

Decodable Words		Automatic Words
Dot	did	a
had	not	was
job	sob	to
mop		of
lots		also
spots		up
globs		get
on		like
top		began
box		

Dot's Job

0   Dot had a job. Dot's job was to mop. She had to mop

13   and mop. Dot had to mop lots of spots. Dot also had to

26   mop up globs. She had to get up on top of a box to mop.

41   Dot did not like to mop. She did not like the job. Dot

54   began to sob and sob.

59

Total Words Read _____

– Errors _____

= CWPM _____

Short "o" Story: Bob the Frog

Decodable Words		Automatic Words
Bob	fond	is
frog		a
hop		who
hopping		likes
on		to
rocks		from
logs		also
plops		then
pond		the
in		of

Bob the Frog

0   Bob is a frog who likes to hop. He is a hopping frog.

13   Bob hops on rocks. He hops from rock to rock. He also

25   hops on logs. Bob hops from log to log.

34   Then Bob plops in the pond. Bob likes to get wet. He

46   is fond of the pond.

51

Total Words Read _____

− Errors _____

= CWPM _____

Short "u" Story: Mutt the Pup

Decodable Words		Automatic Words	
Mutt	had	the	of
pup	sun	is	bath
pet	on	a	he
run	rug	likes	
and	felt	to	
mom	snug	then	
sat	bug	red	
him	fun	as	
in	hug	when	
tub	his	out	

Mutt the Pup

0   Mutt the pup is a fun pet. Mutt likes to run and run.

13   Mutt's mom sat him in the tub. He had a bath in the tub.

27   Then, Mutt sat in the sun on his red rug. He felt as

40   snug as a bug in a rug. Mutt is fun to hug when he is out

56   of the tub.

59

Total Words Read _____

– Errors _____

= CWPM _____

Short "u" Story: Bud the Bug

Decodable Words		Automatic Words
Bud	wet	the
big	had	was
bug	fun	only
in		he
mud		
did		
run		
not		
jog		
dug		

Bud the Bug

0   Bud was a big bug. Bud sat in the mud. He did not

13   run in the mud. He did not jog in the mud. Bud only dug

27   in the mud.

30   Bud dug and dug in the wet mud. He had fun in the

43   mud. Bud was a big bug in the mud.

52

Total Words Read _____

− Errors _____

= CWPM _____

Long "a" Story: Dave and Jake

Decodable Words		Automatic Words
Dave	safe	was
went	gave	the
lake	up	saw
Jake		look
at		looked
snakes		for
in		today
big		to
cave		too
not		

Dave and Jake

0   Dave went to the lake. Jake was at the lake. Dave saw

12   Jake at the lake. Dave was at the lake to look for snakes.

25   Jake was at the lake to look for snakes, too.

35   Dave and Jake went to look for snakes. They looked in

46   a big cave for snakes. It was not safe to look for snakes in

60   the big cave. They gave up. No snakes for Dave and Jake

72   today.

73

Total Words Read _____

− Errors _____

= CWPM _____

Long "a" Story: Kate's Big Cake

Decodable Words		Automatic Words	
Kate	gate	a	you
had	not	was	be
big	at	to	took
cake	ran	would	her
late	up	open	
take	Nate	opened	
bake		face	
sale		now	
came		the	
big		thank	

Kate's Big Cake

0   Kate had a big cake to take to a bake sale. She was

13 late and came to a big gate. The gate would not open. Kate

26 made a face.

29   Nate saw Kate and the big cake at the gate. Nate ran

41 up to Kate. Nate opened the gate. Now Kate and the big

53 cake would not be late. Kate said, "Thank you," to Nate.

64 She took her cake to the bake sale.

72

Total Words Read _____

− Errors _____

= CWPM _____

Long "i" Story: Mike at Camp

Decodable Words		Automatic Words
Mike	ride	for
camp	nine	took
it	mile	long
got	bike	
went		
had		
bikes		
red		
white		
fun		

Mike at Camp

0   It was time for camp. Mike got up and went to camp.

12   The camp had bikes. It had red bikes and white bikes.

23   Mike got a red bike. It was fun to ride the bike.

35   Mike went for a nine-mile bike ride. It took a long

47   time to ride nine miles. Mike liked to ride his red bike. It

60   was fun to go to camp and go on bike rides.

71

Total Words Read _____

– Errors _____

= CWPM _____

Long "i" Story: Cakes and Pies

Decodable Words		Automatic Words	
Kilee	lots	and	she
Mike	fine	were	
bake	baked	was	
bakers	lime	to	
time		all	
liked		the	
limes		so	
pies		they	
rice		of	
cakes		he	

Cakes and Pies

0   Kilee and Mike were bakers. Kilee was Mike's wife.

9   Kilee and Mike liked to bake. They baked all the time.

20   Mike liked limes, so he baked lime pies. Kilee liked

30   rice, so she baked rice cakes. They ate lots of lime pies and

43   rice cakes. They had a fine time.

50

Total Words Read _____

– Errors _____

= CWPM _____

Long "e" Story: The Team

Decodable Words		Automatic Words	
flea	sea	a	so
bee	feed	were	his
pals	team	all	some
helped		four	grass
needed		each	good
and		other	
seal		wanted	
sheep		drink	
hive		of	
tea		find	

The Team

0   A flea and a bee were pals. A seal and a sheep were

13   pals. All four were pals. The four pals helped each other.

24   The bee needed a hive so his pals helped him. The

35   flea wanted a drink of tea. His pals helped him. The seal

47   wanted to find the sea so his pals helped him. The sheep

59   wanted to feed on some grass.

65   All four pals helped each other. The pals were a good

76   team.

77

Total Words Read _____

– Errors _____

= CWPM _____

Long "e" Story: The Mean Queen

Decodable Words	Automatic Words	
Jean	was	books
queen	he	so
nice	very	their
mean	no	not
scream	one	a
green	wanted	she
beans	would	her
red	threw	
beets	cook	
teacher	too	

The Mean Queen

0   Jean was a queen. She was not a nice queen. Jean
11 was a very mean queen. No one wanted to see her. Jean
23 would scream a mean scream. Jean would scream at the
33 cook. She threw green beans at the cook. Jean threw her
44 red beets at the cook, too.
50   Jean was mean to her teacher. Jean did not like to
61 read her books, so she threw them. No one liked mean
72 Jean for a queen. They were sad that she was their queen.
84

Total Words Read _____

− Errors _____

= CWPM _____

Long "o" Story: Joe the Mole

Decodable Words		Automatic Words	
Joe	choked	was	went
mole	pile	a	back
in	stones	who	be
home	poked	wanted	of
did	nose	new	
not	then	want	
stove	ran	lived	
hot	hole	looked	
smoke	fine	too	
made	home	for	

Joe the Mole

0   Joe was a mole who lived in a hole. Joe wanted a new

13 home. He did not want to live in a hole. Joe looked at a

27 stove for a home. The stove was too hot. The smoke made

39 Joe choke.

41   Joe looked at a pile of stones for a new home. Joe

53 poked his nose on the stones. He did not like stones. He

65 went back to his hole. A hole can be a fine home for a

79 mole.

80

Total Words Read _____

− Errors _____

= CWPM _____

Long "o" Story: Rose Rode Horses

Decodable Words	Automatic Words	
Rose	liked	from
rode	horses	she
woke	all	
up	long	
and	day	
flag	each	
pole	end	
zone	way	
whole	to	
home	school	

Rose Rode Horses

0   Rose liked horses. She rode horses. She rode horses all

10   day long. Each day, Rose woke up and rode and rode. She

22   rode to the flag pole. She rode to the end zone.

33   Rose rode the whole way to school. She rode the

43   whole way home from school. Rose rode horses all day

53   long.

54

Total Words Read _____

− Errors _____

= CWPM _____

Long "u" Story: Luke the Mule

Decodable Words	Automatic Words	
Luke	was	sing
mule	lived	when
mules	the	sang
huge	other	they
pen	named	nice
June	care	girl
tunes	took	her
flute	of	with
cute	played	to
	hear	in

Luke the Mule

0   Luke was a nice mule. He lived in a huge pen with

12   other mules. A girl named June took care of the mules.

23   June played tunes on her flute. She played for the mules.

34   Luke liked June's tunes. He liked to hear tunes played

44   on the flute. He liked to sing to the tunes. The other mules

57   liked to sing, too. The mules looked cute when they sang

68   to the tunes.

71

Total Words Read _____

− Errors _____

= CWPM _____

Long "u" Story: The Duke's Mule

Decodable Words	Automatic Words	
Duke	which	he
had	to	so
mule	you	like
ride	say	them
big	don't	only
fell	horse	why
well	not	with
	were	off
	for	on
	this	

The Duke's Mule

0   A duke had a mule on which to ride. A mule, you say!

13 Don't dukes ride on big horses, not mules?

21   Well, horses were not for this duke. He fell off a horse,

33 so he does not like them at all. He likes only mules, so that

47 is why he is a duke with a mule.

56

Total Words Read _____

− Errors _____

= CWPM _____

Practice Passages

First Grade

Level 1: Exercise
101 Keeping Fit
102 Warm Up: Getting Ready
103 Take a Hike
104 Jump Rope
105 Skate Around

Level 1: Insects
106 All about Insects
107 Ants: The Hard Workers
108 Bees: The Busy Workers
109 Fireflies: The Night Workers
110 Ladybugs: The Helpful Workers

Level 1: Pets
111 Pets: Helpful Pals
112 Dogs: Barking Buddies
113 Cats: Purring Pets
114 Birds: Flying Pets
115 Fish: Water Pets

Level 1: Safety
116 Safety Rules and Plans
117 If You Are Lost
118 Fire Safety
119 Bike Safety
120 Walking to School

Level 1: The Sky
121 The Sun, the Moon, and the Stars
122 The Sun
123 The Moon
124 The Stars
125 The Constellations

Second Grade

Level 2: Animal Habitats

Level 2: Citizenship

Level 2: Symbols of Freedom

Level 2: Community Helpers

Level 2: Rain Forests

Third Grade

Level 3: The Human Body

Level 3: Holiday Celebrations

Level 3: Homes of the Past

Level 3: The Solar System

Level 3: Take Care of Waste!

Level 1: Exercise

Vocabulary

exercise: To move your body. To do some kind of physical activity.

muscles: Inside parts of your body that join bones together and help your body move.

stretch: To reach out your arms, legs, or body as far as you can to exercise your muscles.

Keeping Fit

0	Exercise is good for you. There are many reasons why.
10	The best kind of exercise makes you breathe deeply. This
20	helps your lungs grow strong. It gets your heart pumping.
30	This helps your heart grow strong. Swimming is good
39	exercise. So is skating and bike riding. Walking is good for
50	you. So is jumping rope.
55	Some exercise can make you strong. Use your muscles
64	for heavy work. This will make your muscles stronger.
73	Doing push-ups makes you strong. So can bike riding and
84	skating.
85	Exercise makes you flexible. It helps you bend your
94	body. It helps you stretch. Dancing is good. So is karate.
105	Exercise helps stop weight gain. If you are active, you
115	burn off calories. Then your body will not store them as
126	fat.
127	Best of all, keeping fit will make you feel good!
137	

Total Words Read _____

− Errors _____

= CWPM _____

Warm Up: Getting Ready

0   Your body needs to get ready for exercise. The muscles

10   need to warm up. Take time to stretch. Do one stretch at a

23   time. Count to 15. Do each stretch three times.

32   Start with a sit and reach stretch. Sit on the floor. Put

44   your legs out in front of you. Keep your heels on the floor.

57   Stretch your hands to your toes. Hold and count to 15.

68   Next, do a thigh stretch. Roll over. Push yourself up

78   on your hands and knees. Stretch one leg behind you.

88   Then, pull your leg under your chest. Stretch one leg at a

100   time.

101   Now, stand up. Do a back stretch. Lift and then bend

112   your arms. Grab the elbow of one arm. Stretch the elbow

123   down your back as far as you can. Stretch one elbow at a

136   time.

137   Next, stretch your chest. Put your hands behind your

146   back. Hold them together. Pull them slowly back and up.

156   Last, do a leg stretch. Lean against a wall. Bend

166   one leg in front of you. Stretch the other leg behind you.

178   Stretch one leg at a time.

184

Total Words Read _____

− Errors _____

= CWPM _____

Take a Hike

0   Walking is good for you. A fast walk can help your

11   heart. It can also help your lungs. Walking will help your

22   bones be strong. It will help you to be fit.

32   Walking is easy to do. It is fun to walk with someone

44   else. Ask a friend to walk with you. Try to walk fast for 30

58   minutes most days. Fast walking means that you can talk.

68   But you can't sing. You may be puffing a little. Be sure to

81   wear good shoes. Tennis shoes are good walking shoes. Be

91   sure to take water with you on your walk.

100   Stretch your legs before you walk. Start walking

108   slowly. This will warm up your muscles. Then, pick up

118   your speed. At the end of your walk, stretch your muscles

129   again. Walking is a great way to get exercise!

138

Total Words Read _____

– Errors _____

= CWPM _____

Jump Rope

0	Jumping rope is fun. It is also good for you. Jumping
11	rope helps your heart get strong. Your lungs will get
21	strong, too. Jumping rope helps your feet and hands work
31	well together.
33	Be sure to wear good shoes. You will need shoes that
44	support your feet. Always jump on flat ground. Start out
54	slowly.
55	Start with your hands beside your body. Keep your
64	arms straight. Keep them relaxed. Jump on both feet. Land
74	on the balls of your feet. Jump once for each turn of the
87	rope. Be sure to keep your feet together. Keep your ankles
98	and knees together, too. Learn to jump low. Learn to jump
109	soft. Learn to jump standing straight up.
116	Keep track of how many times you jump. Start with 30
127	hops. Then, add some hops. Keep track of how long you
138	jump. Add one minute each week.
144	

Total Words Read _____

– Errors _____

= CWPM _____

Skate Around

0   Skating is good exercise. It is fun, too. But skating is

11   not easy. There are tools to buy. There are rules to learn.

23   You must know what to do before you put wheels on your

35   feet.

36   If you want to be a skater, you will need skates. The

48   skates must fit well. You will also need a helmet. It is good

61   to have knee pads. Elbow pads are also good. Some skaters

72   wear gloves.

74   Skaters can be dangerous. Skaters must know how

82   to use their skates. They need to know how to get going.

94   They need to know how to stop. Skaters fall down. You

105   must know safe ways to fall.

111   Learn to skate where there is no traffic. Look for flat

122   roads. Stay away from rocks and holes. The best place to

133   skate is in a park.

138

Total Words Read _____

\- Errors _____

= CWPM _____

Level 1: Insects

Vocabulary

egg: A round object with a hard shell that is laid by a female. An egg grows into an animal.

insect: A very small animal with six legs and three main body parts. Most insects have wings.

larva: An insect when it first hatches from an egg. A larva looks like a worm.

pupa: A stage in the life cycle of an insect. The time when a larva changes into an adult.

All About Insects

0   An insect is a tiny animal. It has six legs. It has a

13   body. An insect's body has three parts. Most insects have

23   wings. Insects do not have a backbone.

30   There are more than one million kinds of insects. They

40   are found all over. Insects can live in hot places. They can

52   live in cold places. There are many kinds of insects. Insects

63   do not look alike. They come in many colors. They also

74   come in many shapes.

78   Insects have a life cycle. Each insect starts life as an

89   egg. The egg hatches. It becomes a larva. A larva looks like

101 a worm. It has a mouth. But it does not have eyes. A larva

115 likes to eat. It eats and eats. The larva gets very big. Then,

128 it is too big for its skin. The larva sheds its skin. Later,

141 the larva spins a cocoon. It lives in the cocoon. Now it is

154 called a pupa. After a while, the pupa leaves its cocoon.

165 Then, it is an adult insect.

171

Total Words Read _____

– Errors _____

= CWPM _____

Ants: The Hard Workers

0	Ants are insects. Most ants live in the soil. They live
11	in nests. Their nests are called colonies. Each colony has
21	many ants. The colonies have a lot of rooms. Ants take
32	care of their colonies. They keep food in their colonies.
42	Each ant has a job. Some ants care for the nest. Others
54	look for food. When they find food, they make a trail.
65	Other ants find the trail. They carry the food to the nest.
77	Each nest has one queen ant. The queen stays in the
88	nest. She lays eggs. Each egg grows to be a larva. A larva
101	is white. It looks like a worm. It has no eyes or legs. But
115	it does have a mouth. The ants feed each larva. The larva
127	grows. It wraps into a cocoon. The larva changes in the
138	cocoon. It grows into an adult ant.
145	

Total Words Read _____

− Errors _____

= CWPM _____

Bees: The Busy Workers

0	Bees are insects. They have four wings. The bees'
9	wings move very fast. The wings make a buzzing sound.
19	Bees live in a hive. A hive is made of cells. The cells are
33	made of wax. Each hive has one queen bee. But it has
45	many worker bees. Worker bees are little. But they are
55	hard workers. They each have a job.
62	The queen bee has only one job. Her job is to lay
74	eggs. Each egg hatches into a larva. Worker bees feed the
85	larva. Each larva makes a cocoon. Then the larva turns
95	into a pupa. The pupa turns into an adult bee.
105	Worker bees have other jobs. Some guard the hive.
114	Some keep the hive cool. Others take nectar from flowers.
124	Bees use nectar. They turn it into honey. The honey is put
136	into the hive. It is kept in the wax cells. Bees use honey for
150	food. Bees make more honey than they can use. Honey is
161	very sweet. People like honey, too.
167	

Total Words Read _____

− Errors _____

= CWPM _____

The Six-Minute Solution: A Reading Fluency Program (Primary Level)

Fireflies: The Night Workers

0	Fireflies are insects. But they are not flies. They are a
11	kind of beetle. Fireflies have a hard shell. The shell covers
22	their wings. Fireflies live in the grass. They eat small bugs.
33	They also eat snails.
37	Fireflies have a big tail. Their tail makes a yellow
47	light. They fly on warm nights. When they fly at night,
58	they look like little lights in the air. Fireflies talk to each
70	other using their tails. They flash light patterns to each
80	other. Fireflies go to sleep about 9 p.m. When they go to
92	sleep, their lights fade.
96	In the fall, fireflies lay eggs. They lay eggs on leaves.
107	Rain washes the eggs to the soil. Each egg hatches into
118	a larva. A larva stays in the soil all winter. Then spring
130	comes. The larva comes out to feed. In the summer, it
142	turns into a pupa. It stays a pupa for about two weeks.
153	Then it becomes an adult firefly.
159	

Total Words Read _____

− Errors _____

= CWPM _____

Ladybugs: The Helpful Workers

0	Ladybugs are insects. They are pretty. Their wings
8	are red. They are shiny. The wings have black dots. These
19	bugs are a kind of beetle.
25	People like ladybugs. The bugs are helpful. They eat
34	aphids. Aphids are pests that eat plants. When there are no
45	aphids, plants grow. Their flowers are pretty. Their fruit is
55	good to eat. Ladybugs are good for plants. People like to
66	have these bugs in their yards.
72	Ladybugs lay many eggs. The eggs are very tiny.
81	Each egg hatches. It becomes a larva. The larva is little
92	and long. It looks like a worm. The larva sticks to a plant.
105	Then the larva splits open. A pupa comes out. It is in a
118	cocoon. Soon, the pupa comes out of the cocoon. It is now
130	a ladybug.
132	

Total Words Read _____

− Errors _____

= CWPM _____

Level 1: Pets

Vocabulary

care: To give pets what they need (for example, food, water, and a safe place to sleep).

pet: An animal that lives at home.

special care: More care than usual. Care that is given for an important reason.

Pets: Helpful Pals

0	Pets are animals that live with people. Pets are fun to
11	have around. We like to play with them. Pets are fun to
23	touch. We can talk to our pets. They make us feel happy.
35	But pets also help us. They help us learn. Pets need
46	us to give them food. They need us to give them water. We
59	have to take care of our pets. If we don't take care of them,
73	they could get sick or die. We have to remember to care for
86	pets every day. That helps us learn to be responsible.
96	Being in charge of a pet helps us to learn other things.
108	Pets need to be safe. We must watch them. Some pets
119	must stay inside. If they go outside, they could get hurt.
130	We must keep them from danger. Watching pets helps us
140	to learn to pay attention.
145	Taking care of pets is a lot of work. Sometimes, pets
156	do not do what we want them to do. We may have to fix
170	their mistakes. That helps us learn to be patient.
179	We have a lot of fun with pets. But we also learn from
192	them! Pets are good for people!
198	

Total Words Read _____

\- Errors _____

= CWPM _____

The Six-Minute Solution: A Reading Fluency Program (Primary Level)

Dogs: Barking Buddies

0	Dogs are good pets. But they are a lot of work. Be sure
13	that you are ready to take good care of a dog. There are
26	more than 400 kinds of dogs. Some are very small. Others
37	are very big. Pick the kind of dog that is right for you and
51	your family.
53	Dogs need food and water in a clean dish every day.
64	They need shelter from bad weather. Dogs must have
73	exercise. They like to go for walks. Their hair must be
84	brushed often. They need to go to the vet for check-ups
96	and shots.
98	Dogs must learn how to behave. You will have to
108	spend time training your dog. Dogs need love. They like to
119	be around people. You must spend time playing with your
129	dog every day.
132	Taking care of a dog can be hard work. But a dog will
145	be your best friend for many years to come.
154	

Total Words Read _____

− Errors _____

= CWPM _____

Cats: Purring Pets

0   Cats are good pets. Like all pets, they need special

10   care. Cats need food and water every day. Cats are meat

21   eaters. They must have meat every day. Give your cat food

32   made from beef, chicken, or fish. Cats do not need to drink

44   milk. Give your cat fresh water.

50   Cats need a safe place to live. Cats that live indoors

61   are safer than cats that live outdoors. If you let your cat

73   outside, be sure it is in the daytime. At night, wild animals

85   can attack a cat.

89   Cats use litter boxes. You need to keep your cat's litter

100   box clean. It must be cleaned at least once a day. Cats like

113   clean litter boxes.

116   Play with your cat every day. Playing keeps them from

126   getting bored. It is also good exercise. Remember to take

136   your cat to the vet for check-ups. A healthy cat will have a

150   long life.

152

Total Words Read _____

- Errors _____

= CWPM _____

Birds: Flying Pets

0	Birds make good pets. There are many kinds of birds.
10	Like all pets, birds need special care. Birds must be treated
21	gently. Some birds like to be held. Others do not. Many
32	birds sing. Others can talk.
37	Birds need cages. The cage should be large enough for
47	the bird to fly around. Flying is good exercise. Put perches
58	in the cage. Birds like to jump on perches. Put paper in the
71	bottom of the cage. The paper must be changed every day.
82	Put the cage in a warm place. The kitchen is not a good
95	place for birds. They can get sick from oven fumes.
105	Birds eat special food. Buy the right kind at a pet
116	store. Make sure that your bird always has food. Birds
126	need water to drink. All birds love to take baths. Give your
138	bird two cups of water. One is to drink. The other is for
151	bathing. It is fun to watch birds splash in their bath.
162	With good care, birds can live for many years.
171	

Total Words Read _____

\- Errors _____

= CWPM _____

Fish: Water Pets

0	There are many kinds of fish. Some live in cold water.
11	Others live in warm water.
16	Goldfish make good pets. They live in cold water. It
26	is easier to take care of coldwater fish. Goldfish are fun to
38	watch. They like to jump. They also like to splash.
48	Goldfish become excited when it is meal time. They
57	swim very fast. Goldfish eat special fish food. They also
67	eat vegetables. Peas are good for goldfish.
74	Like all pets, goldfish need special care. You will need
84	to have a big fish tank for your fish. There should be a
97	lid on the tank. The lid will keep the fish safe inside. Do
110	not put too many fish together in one tank. Goldfish need
121	room to grow.
124	Goldfish, like other fish, need clean water in their
133	tank. You will need to clean the fish tank often.
143	If you take good care of your goldfish, it will live for
155	many years.
157	

Total Words Read _____

\- Errors _____

= CWPM _____

Level 1: Safety

Vocabulary

careful: To think as you do something to avoid danger.

danger: Something that can hurt you.

plan: To prepare to do something in the future.

safe: Not in danger.

Safety Plans and Rules

0   Children need to know how to be safe. They need to

11   know what to do if they are afraid. If children know what

23   to do, they can help themselves. They can try to keep out

35   of danger.

37   Adults teach children to be safe. They teach children

46   to stop and think. They teach children to have a plan.

57   Children need to have many plans. Having plans will help

67   them know what to do. Children need to know what to do

79   if they are lost. They need to know what to do if there is a

94   fire.

95   Children also need to know rules. Rules can keep

104   them safe. Children need to know the rules for crossing the

115   street. They need to know rules for bike riding.

124

Total Words Read _____

– Errors _____

= CWPM _____

If You Are Lost

0	Sometimes, children get lost. If you get lost, don't be
10	scared. Stop and think about a plan. If you are lost in the
23	woods, find a tree. Stay by the tree. Hug the tree. Do not
36	move to another place. People will be looking for you. If
47	you move, they may not find you. Stay in one place. Give
59	people time to find you.
64	If you are lost in a city, look for help. Look for the
77	police. Do not talk to strangers. Look for a telephone. Dial
88	911. You do not need money to call. Tell the adult on the
101	phone that you are lost. The adult will send the police to
113	find you. The police will take you to your family.
123	

Total Words Read _____

\- Errors _____

= CWPM _____

Fire Safety

0	Be safe about fire. Fire can cause danger. Never play
10	with matches. Never play with lighters. Stay away from the
20	stove. Do not try to cook alone.
27	If your clothes catch on fire, do not run. Running will
38	make the fire get bigger. Remember to stop, drop, and roll.
49	What does this mean? Stop right away. Fall to the ground.
60	Then roll around on the ground. This will help to put out
72	the fire.
74	If you see a fire, find a phone. Dial 911. Tell the adult
87	on the phone about the fire. Do not hang up the phone.
99	Listen and do what the adult tells you to do. The adult will
112	send help. A fire truck will come.
119	

Total Words Read _____

– Errors _____

= CWPM _____

Bike Safety

0   Riding a bike is fun. Children like to ride bikes. They

11   need to be careful. They need to follow the rules. Wear a

23   helmet. If you fall off your bike, you could hurt your head.

35   A helmet helps to make sure that your head is not hurt.

47   Ride your bike on the right side of the street. This is

59   same way that cars go. A car does not expect to see a bike

73   coming toward them. Stay in the bike lane. Do not ride on

85   the part of the road where cars go. A car could hit a bike.

99   Learn the hand signals. The signals let the cars know

109 if you are going to turn. If you want to turn left, make the

123 left turn signal. If you want to turn right, make the right

135 turn signal.

137 You can have fun riding a bike. But be sure to be safe!

150

Total Words Read _____

− Errors _____

= CWPM _____

Walking to School

0   Many children walk to school. They need to know

9 safety rules. The rules will keep them safe.

17   Have a plan when you walk to school. Pick a way

28 with few streets to cross. Walk the same way to school

39 every day. Do not walk alone. Walk with a friend. Do not

51 stop to play on the way to school or home.

61   Do not talk to strangers. A stranger is someone you

71 do not know. Never take a ride from a stranger. If someone

83 asks you to get in a car, yell "NO!" Then, run away.

95   Look both ways before you cross the street. Do not

105 cross in the middle of the street. Go to a safe street corner.

118 Obey the traffic signs. Watch for turning cars. Do not run.

129 Always walk across the street. Do not walk between cars

139 that are parked in the street or in a parking lot.

150   You can have fun walking to school. But be sure to be

162 safe!

163

Total Words Read _____

- Errors _____

= CWPM _____

Level 1: The Sky

Vocabulary

constellations: Groups of stars that make patterns and have names.

moon: A bright ball of rock and dust that appears in the night sky.

stars: Points of light in the night sky.

sun: A large, bright star in the sky that gives off light and heat.

The Sun, the Moon, and the Stars

0	We see the sun every day. It looks like it is moving.
12	But the sun does not really move. It is the Earth that is
25	moving. The Earth moves around the sun. This movement
34	makes days and nights. It also makes seasons.
42	We see the moon at night. It is the biggest object in
54	the night sky. The moon looks like it shines. But it does
66	not really give off light. The light from the moon comes
77	from the sun. The moon moves around the Earth. As it
88	moves, the moon changes shape.
93	We see stars at night. They look like small points of
104	light. Stars look small because they are far away. But stars
115	are really big. They are bigger than the Earth.
124	

Total Words Read _____

– Errors _____

= CWPM _____

The Sun

0	The sun is a star. It is the closest star to Earth. It is
4	93 million miles away from Earth. The sun looks small
24	because it is far away. But the sun is much bigger than
36	Earth.
37	The sun is made of gases. The gases are very hot. The
49	sun gives off light. Light is a kind of energy. The sun lights
62	up the Earth. Plants need the sun's light to grow. They
73	need the sun's light to make food.
80	The sun also gives off heat. The heat from the sun
91	warms the land. It also warms the water and the air. The
103	sun's heat warms all living things on Earth.
111	The sun is important to life on Earth. It gives us light
123	and heat. The light and heat from the sun is called solar
135	energy.
136	

Total Words Read _____

− Errors _____

= CWPM _____

The Moon

0	We can see the moon at night. It is a huge ball. The
13	moon is made of rock and dust. It looks like it has spots
26	on it. These spots are holes. The holes are called craters.
37	They are made when a rock flies through space and hits
48	the moon.
50	The moon is the Earth's satellite. That means that the
60	moon moves around the Earth. It takes the moon about
70	one month to orbit the Earth.
76	When it starts, the moon is between the sun and
86	Earth. We can't see the moon from Earth then. One week
97	later, the moon is one-fourth of the way around the Earth.
109	It looks like a half-circle in the night sky. In two weeks,
122	the moon is halfway around. It looks like a full circle from
134	Earth. In three weeks, the moon is three-fourths of the way
146	around the Earth. By the fourth week, the moon is back
157	where it started.
160	

Total Words Read _____

− Errors _____

= CWPM _____

The Stars

0	Stars are big, glowing balls. They are made of hot
10	gases. The hot gases give off light. We can see the light
22	from Earth.
24	Stars look bright. Some stars look brighter than others.
33	Bigger stars look brighter than smaller stars. Stars that are
43	hotter look brighter. The closer the stars are to Earth, the
54	brighter they look.
57	Stars also seem to twinkle. We see stars through layers
67	of moving air. It seems like the stars move a bit. Stars
79	that twinkle more are close to the Earth's horizon. That is
90	because they have to travel through more air. Stars that are
101	overhead do not twinkle as much.
107	The sun is a star. It is a medium-size star. The sun is
121	the closest star to Earth.
126	

Total Words Read _____

- Errors _____

= CWPM _____

The Constellations

0	Some stars are in groups. From Earth, they form a
10	pattern. A star pattern is called a constellation. The night
20	sky has about 88 constellations.
25	One is the Big Dipper. The Big Dipper is a group of
37	seven stars. These seven stars form a dipper. A dipper is a
49	big spoon. It looks like a gravy ladle. Three stars form the
61	handle. Four stars form the cup.
67	The Big Dipper is easy to find in the night sky. This
79	is because its stars are very bright. The best time to see
91	the Big Dipper is in the middle of summer. Look in the
103	northern sky. First, find the handle. Then it will be easy to
115	see the cup.
118	We can use the Big Dipper to find other things in the
130	sky. The two stars on the front of its cup line up with the
144	Little Dipper. The Little Dipper is smaller than the Big
154	Dipper. Its cup hangs down from its handle. Look for a
165	bright star at the end of the Little Dipper's handle. That is
177	the North Star. When we look at it, we know that we are
190	facing north.
192	

Total Words Read _____

− Errors _____

= CWPM _____

Level 2: Animal Habitats

Vocabulary

animal: A creature of nature (not a person or a plant).

food: Something that is eaten.

habitat: A place where an animal lives or a plant grows.

land: The solid part of the earth.

refuge: A safe place.

temperature: The degree of heat or cold.

water: The liquid part of the earth (such as lakes, rivers, and seas).

Animal Habitats Introduction

0   A habitat is a home for an animal. There are many

11   kinds of habitats. The earth has 16 habitats. Some are

21   on land. Some are in water. Habitats have a range of

32   temperatures. They can be very cold. They can be very

42   hot. Most animals can live in only one or two kinds of

54   habitats. A whale cannot live on land, nor can a polar bear

66   live in the desert.

70   Habitats have what animals need. They have food.

78   They have water. Habitats have hiding places. They have

87   places to make nests. Habitats protect animals from cold or

97   heat.

98   Sometimes, animals move from one habitat to another.

106 They do this in the spring. Then, they move again in the

118 fall. They may move to find a warmer habitat. Or they may

130 move to find more food.

135

Total Words Read _____

– Errors _____

= CWPM _____

Ocean Habitats

0	Oceans cover much of our Earth. About 70% of the
10	Earth is water. Oceans have four parts. They are habitat
20	zones. The first zone is near the top of the ocean. The
32	second zone goes down 1,000 meters. The third zone goes
42	down to 4,000 meters. The last zone is the ocean floor.
53	Many animals live in the ocean. Billions of fish live in
64	the ocean. There are more than 25,000 kinds of fish. Some
75	are tiny, and some are huge. They have many colors. Most
86	fish live in water that is close to the shore. They live in
99	water that is less than 600 feet deep. Some fish live in the
112	deep part of the ocean. There is less light in deep water.
124	Some of these fish glow in the dark.
132	Other kinds of animals live in the ocean. Mammals
141	live in oceans. A whale is an ocean mammal. So is a
153	dolphin. They live in the water, but they swim to the top
165	to breathe air. Reptiles also live in the ocean. A sea turtle
177	is an ocean reptile. It also breathes air. When a sea turtle is
190	resting, it can stay underwater for up to two hours. Ocean
201	zones are habitats for many animals.
207	

Total Words Read _____

- Errors _____

= CWPM _____

Desert Habitats

0   Deserts are very dry lands. They do not have much

10   water. The temperature in a desert is both hot and cold.

21   Deserts are very hot in the daytime. But, they can become

32   very cold at night. There are many deserts. They are all

43   over the world. Deserts make up one-fifth of the Earth's

54   land.

55   It is hard to live in the desert. Many desert animals

66   sleep during the day. They do this to stay out of the desert

79   heat. These animals come out at dawn or dusk. Some

89   desert animals dig holes under the ground. They stay in

99   these holes during the hot part of the day. Other desert

110   animals like lizards do not sleep during the day. Lizards

120   have long legs. They have bodies that are close to the

131   ground. This helps them stay cool.

137   Many desert animals do not need much water. The

146   ones that do need water can get it from plants. A cactus is

159   a desert plant. It stores water. Animals can get water from

170   inside a cactus.

173

Total Words Read _____

− Errors _____

= CWPM _____

Habitat Help

0	Some animals are in trouble. There are not many
9	of them left. They are endangered. These animals may
18	become extinct. Then they will be gone forever.
26	How does this happen? One way is if the animal loses
37	its home. An animal needs a special place to live. These
48	places are habitats. Habitats have what the animal needs.
57	They have food. They have water. Habitats have hiding
66	places. They have places to make nests. Habitats protect
75	animals from cold or heat. Animals die if they do not have
87	the right habitat.
90	People need to help save habitats. We can make
99	special places for animals. Wildlife refuges are safe places.
108	So are national parks. We can recycle trash. We can stop
119	using bad chemicals in our gardens. Then they will not
129	end up in animal habitats. We can turn off lights and the
141	TV when we are not using them. This will save energy. We
153	can turn off the water while we brush our teeth. This will
165	save water.
167	We can all do our part to help save animal habitats.
178	

Total Words Read _____

- Errors _____

= CWPM _____

Wildlife Refuges

0	There are special homes for animals. They are safe
9	places. These places are refuges. Refuges are on public
18	land. They belong to the people.
24	The U.S. set up refuges. The first was in Florida. It
35	was set up in 1903. That was more than 100 years ago. It
48	is a refuge for birds and turtles. There are 530 refuges in
60	the U.S. today. Each state has one. Some states have more
71	than one.
73	People work in refuges. They work for the U.S. Their
83	job is to watch out for the animals. The people are refuge
95	managers. They visit the refuges every day. They look for
105	animals. They count the ones they see. The people look for
116	animal tracks. They count the tracks. If an animal is hurt,
127	the managers help.
130	

Total Words Read _____

− Errors _____

= CWPM _____

The Six-Minute Solution: A Reading Fluency Program (Primary Level)

Level 2: Citizenship

Vocabulary

citizen: Someone who lives in a certain city, state, or country.

government: A group of people who control the laws of a city, state, or country.

law: A system of rules that people in a city, state, or country must obey.

tax: Money that citizens pay to a government.

vote: To mark a paper or to raise your hand to show which law or person you want to choose.

Citizens

0   People belong to groups. A family is a group. A class

11   is a group. Friends are a group. Citizens are a group, too.

23   They were born in a country. They belong to that country.

34   People born in the U.S. are U.S. citizens. Some U.S.

44   citizens live in another country. They have children born

53   in that country. The children will be U.S. citizens, too.

63   People come to the U.S. from other countries. They

72   are looking for a better life. The U.S. is made up of people

85   from different countries. That is why the U.S. is called the

96   "melting pot." People born in another country can become

105   U.S. citizens. They have to do three things. First, they

115   must apply to be a U.S. citizen. Then, they must pass a

127   test. Finally, they talk to a judge. The judge decides if the

139   person can be a U.S. citizen.

145

Total Words Read _____

− Errors _____

= CWPM _____

The Right to Vote

0   U.S. citizens are lucky. They have a lot of freedom.

10   They have many rights. Voting is an important right. When

20   people vote, they choose what they want. People in groups

30   may want different things. Voting is a fair way to decide.

41   Families sometimes vote. They might vote on what to

50   have for dinner. Classes sometimes vote. They might vote

59   on what to do after lunch. Friends can vote. They might

70   vote on which movie to see.

76   In the U.S., citizens who are 18 years or older can

87   vote. They can vote for the people they want to be their

99   leaders. They can vote for the president of the U.S. It is

111   important for citizens to vote.

116

Total Words Read _____

− Errors _____

= CWPM _____

The Laws of the Land

0	People in groups work together. They also play
8	together. People in groups have to get along with each
18	other. People get along when they follow rules. Some rules
28	tell what to do. Other rules tell what not to do.
39	Laws are rules that people must obey. Laws are made
49	to help solve problems. They are also made to help stop
60	problems. Many laws are made to keep people safe. All
70	countries have laws. People are expected to follow the
79	laws.
80	In the U.S., people are expected to follow many laws.
90	They must obey the laws in their city. They must obey the
102	laws in their state. All U.S. citizens must obey the laws of
114	the country. They must respect each other's rights. U.S.
123	citizens must pay taxes. Taxes are money that people pay
133	to their country. Tax money is used to pay for things the
145	country needs.
147	

Total Words Read _____

− Errors _____

= CWPM _____

Our Country's Government

0   Our country has a government. It is a group of

10   people. They are the people in charge. In the U.S., citizens

21   vote. They choose their leaders. These leaders are the

30   government.

31   The first U.S. leaders wrote a plan. The plan is the

42   U.S. Constitution. It lists all of the most important laws.

52   It begins with famous words: " We the people of the

62   United States." The Constitution also lists the rights of

71   U.S. citizens. We have many rights. One is the freedom to

82   worship in our own way. Another is the right to vote.

93   Washington, D.C., is a city. It is the U.S. capital city.

104 It is an important place. Our government is there. Our

114 top leaders are there. The president lives there. The city

124 was named for George Washington. He was the first U.S.

134 president.

135

Total Words Read _____

- Errors _____

= CWPM _____

How to Be a Good Citizen

0   What does it take to be a good citizen? One way is to
13   be honest. Honest people tell the truth. They are honest
23   with themselves. They are also honest with other people.

32   Good citizens care. They care about themselves. They
40   care about each other. Good citizens care about the world.

50   Good citizens show respect. That means that they are
59   polite. They obey the law. They respect themselves. They
68   respect other people, too.

72   Good citizens are responsible. They do what they say
81   they will do. They don't make excuses. They don't blame
91   other people.

93   Good citizens are brave. They are brave enough to do
103   the right thing. They are also brave enough to ask for help
115   when they need it.

119   We are lucky to have many good citizens in our world.
130

Total Words Read _____

\- Errors _____

= CWPM _____

Level 2: Symbols of Freedom

Vocabulary

America: A country. Also called *the United States*.

freedom: The right to do whatever you want to do. To not be controlled by someone else.

symbol: A picture, person, or object that stands for a thing or an idea.

United States: A country made up of 50 states. Also called *America*.

Symbols of Freedom Introduction

0   A symbol stands for something. It is special. A symbol

10   puts a picture in our mind. Symbols are all around us. A

22   heart can be a symbol. When we see a heart, it can mean

35   love. It could also mean a valentine. A symbol can mean a

47   sound. A music note is a symbol.

54   The U.S. has symbols. They stand for our country.

63   They stand for U.S. ideas. They stand for freedom. Our

73   flag is a symbol. An animal can also be a symbol. The bald

86   eagle is a U.S. symbol. A building can be a symbol. The

98   White House is a U.S. symbol. A statue can be a symbol.

110   The Statue of Liberty is a symbol. Symbols are important.

120

Total Words Read _____

− Errors _____

= CWPM _____

The American Flag

0	The American flag is a symbol. It stands for our
10	country. The flag is a symbol of unity. It is also a symbol
23	of strength. The colors of the flag are red, white, and blue.
35	The colors are also symbols. Red is a symbol for hardiness.
46	It also means valor. White is a symbol for purity. It also
58	means innocence. Blue is a symbol for justice.
66	The American flag has 13 stars and stripes. The stripes
76	are red and white. There are 7 red stripes and 6 white
88	stripes. The stripes are symbols for the first 13 states. The
99	flag has a group of stars. The stars are white on a blue
112	background. Each star is a symbol for a state. A star is
124	added each time a state joins the U.S. Today, the flag has
136	50 stars.
138	

Total Words Read _____

− Errors _____

= CWPM _____

The White House

0	The White House is a U.S. symbol. It is in
10	Washington, D.C. The White House is a symbol of the
20	president. It is also a symbol of our government.
29	The president lives in the White House. His family
38	lives there, too. They have a private living space. The
48	president also works in the White House. He works in the
59	Oval Office. The Oval Office is in the West Wing of the
71	White House.
73	The White House is a very large and famous place.
83	It has 132 rooms. Many people come to visit the White
94	House each year. The White House has a gym. It also has a
107	movie theatre. There are tennis courts and a bowling alley,
117	too.
118	The president gives speeches from the Oval Office.
126	People watch these speeches on TV.
132	

Total Words Read _____

– Errors _____

= CWPM _____

The Bald Eagle

0	The bald eagle is a symbol of the United States. It is
12	our country's bird. Eagles are symbols of strength. They
21	are also symbols of bravery.
26	The bald eagle is a strong bird. It is also majestic.
37	That is why it was picked to be a U.S. symbol. The eagle
50	is not really bald. It has white feathers on top of its head.
63	The feathers are hard to see. So the eagle looks bald even
75	though it is not.
79	In 1782, Congress put the bald eagle on the Great
89	Seal. The Great Seal is the stamp of the United States.
100	

Total Words Read _____

− Errors _____

= CWPM _____

The Statue of Liberty

0   The Statue of Liberty is a U.S. symbol. It is in New

12   York Harbor. It is one of the largest statues in the world.

24   France gave "Lady Liberty" to the U.S. It was a gift of

36   friendship.

37   The Statue of Liberty has a crown on its head. The

48   crown has seven rays. The rays stand for the seven seas.

59   The rays also stand for the seven continents. The statue

69   holds a torch in one hand. The torch is a symbol of

81   welcome. It welcomes people who come to America.

89   The statue holds a tablet in the other hand. The date

100 on the tablet is July 4, 1776. That was the day the U.S.

113 became a country.

116

Total Words Read _____

− Errors _____

= CWPM _____

Level 2: Community Helpers

Vocabulary

community: A place that has many different neighborhoods.

doctors: People whose job it is to take care of sick people.

fire fighters: People whose job it is to put out fires.

neighborhood: A small area of a town and/or the people who live there.

police officers: People whose job it is to protect others and make sure that people obey laws.

teachers: People whose job it is to help others learn.

A Community

0   A community is a place. It has neighborhoods. A

9   community can be small. It can also be big. It is where

21 people live. There are many kinds of people. Some are

31 families. Others are single. Some are old people. Others are

41 young.

42   People work in a community. They have many jobs.

51 Some work in stores. Others work in offices. Many have

61 special jobs. Their jobs are to help people. Fire fighters

71 have helping jobs. So do police officers. Teachers have

80 helping jobs. So do doctors.

85   A community is special. Each one is different. It has

95 special places. There are special things to do. But some

105 things are the same. People work together. They play

114 together. They help each other.

119

Total Words Read _____

– Errors _____

= CWPM _____

Fire Fighters

0   Fire fighters are very brave. They run into burning

9   places. They put out fires. They save lives. Fire fighters are

20   not only brave. They are strong. They are healthy. They

30   go up and down ladders. Sometimes, they have to carry

40   people.

41   Fire fighters wear special clothes. Their clothes are

49   made to keep them safe. They are fire-resistant. Their

59   pants and coats are called "turnouts." Turnout pants are

68   turned inside out when fire fighters roll them down over

78   their boots. The boots are hooked onto the rolled-down

88   pants. Fire fighters can jump into their boots. Then, they

98   pull up their pants, right side out. They can get to a fire

111 quickly.

112   Fire fighter boots have handles on the top. The

121 handles help fire fighters get their boots on. Fire fighters

131 wear face masks. The masks help them to breathe in hot

142 and smoky places. They wear helmets and gloves, too.

151   Fire fighters use many tools to help them with their

161 job. They have fire hoses. The hoses are strong and help to

173 put out fires. Fire fighters also have axes. Axes help them

184 get into burning buildings.

188

Total Words Read _____

− Errors _____

= CWPM _____

Police Officers

0	Police officers have a special job. They make sure
9	that people follow laws. Some laws tell people what to do.
20	Other laws tell people what not to do. A law is a rule that
34	all people must follow. Police officers enforce laws. They
43	try to keep people from doing the wrong thing. Sometimes,
53	people do bad things. They break laws. Police officers
62	catch them.
64	The police keep people safe. They watch the streets.
73	They also watch the highways. Police officers take care of
83	people. They help people who are hurt. They help people
93	who are lost. The police walk neighborhood streets. They
102	make sure that everyone and everything are safe.
110	Police officers wear uniforms. They carry a badge.
118	They use special tools. A whistle is a tool. So is a two-way
132	radio. Handcuffs are tools, too. Police officers carry guns.
141	They are trained in how to use guns and follow gun safety
153	rules.
154	

Total Words Read _____

- Errors _____

= CWPM _____

Doctors

0	Doctors help people who are sick or hurt. They try
10	to find out what is wrong. They ask questions. Doctors
20	may order blood tests. They may order X-rays. Doctors
30	tell people what the tests and X-rays mean. Doctors help
41	people to feel better. They may give medicine. Sometimes,
50	they may operate.
53	Doctors need special tools. One tool helps them to
62	listen to people's lungs. Another tool is used to check
72	people's eyes. Doctors use a different tool to look into ears.
83	They use another tool to check blood pressure.
91	Doctors also help people who are well. They give
100	people check-ups. Doctors tell people how to stay healthy.
110	They talk about diet. They also talk about exercise. It is
121	important to visit the doctor for check-ups.
129	

Total Words Read _____

− Errors _____

= CWPM _____

Teachers

0	Teachers are important. They help students learn.
7	Teachers help them understand. Students spend a lot
15	of time in school. They spend many hours with their
25	teachers.
26	There are all kinds of teachers. Some teach young
35	children. Some work with teenagers. Others teach at
43	colleges. Teachers work with many kinds of students. All
52	students learn in their own way. Some learn by seeing.
62	Others learn by hearing. Many students learn by doing.
71	Some students learn easily. Others have trouble learning.
79	Teachers have to know many ways to teach.
87	Teachers have special tools. Some use chalkboards.
94	They write with chalk. Others use dry erase boards.
103	They write with markers. Many teachers use overhead
111	projectors. Others use computers. Some teachers use
118	videos or music.
121	Teachers work very hard. They are always learning.
129	They pass on what they learn to their students. When
139	students learn, they feel good about themselves.
146	

Total Words Read _____

– Errors _____

= CWPM _____

Level 2: Rain Forests

Vocabulary

animals: Living creatures (such as bears, monkeys, and dogs).

nature: Everything in the world that is not human.

plants: Living things with roots, branches, and leaves.

rain forests: Thick forests with tall trees that grow very closely together.

temperate: An environment that is mild and comfortable.

tropical: An environment that is hot and wet.

Rain Forests: Nature's Friends

0   There are two kinds of rain forests. One kind is a

11   tropical rain forest. Tropical rain forests are in warm

20   places. The other kind is a temperate rain forest.

29   Temperate rain forests are in cooler places.

36   Rain forests are thick with trees. They are also wet

46   places. It is always raining in a rain forest. Lots of plants

58   and animals live in rain forests.

64   Rain forests have four zones, or layers. The top layer

74   is the tops of giant trees. It is called the *emergent* zone.

86   Birds and insects live there. The next zone is called the

97   *canopy*. It is the upper part of the trees. Many kinds of

109   animals live in the canopy. The *understory* is the next

119   zone. It is the lower layer of the forest that has a lot of

133   plants and small animals. It is dark and cool. The last zone

145   is the *forest floor*. Insects and large animals live there.

155   Rain forests are important to the world. Rain forest

164   plants make a lot of the earth's oxygen. They also take

175   carbon dioxide out of the air and store it in their roots.

187   This helps to keep the earth cooler. Rain forest plants are

198   used to make medicine. These drugs help people fight

207   diseases. Rain forests also clean and recycle water for the

217   earth.

218   Rain forests are in danger. People are cutting down

227   trees in rain forests to make wood and paper. Rain forests

238   need our help. We must ask people to stop cutting down

249   rain forest trees.

252

Total Words Read _____

− Errors _____

= CWPM _____

Animals of the Rain Forest

0	Many animals live in rain forests. They live in all
10	layers of the rain forests. Birds live in the emergent layer.
21	They live in the giant trees. Birds also live in the canopy.
33	It is the upper part of the trees. The toucan is a rain forest
47	bird. Its beak is large and colorful.
54	Amphibians live in rain forests. They spend part of
63	their time in water. The rest of the time, they spend on
75	land. The red-eyed frog is a rain forest animal. It has bright
80	red eyes.
90	Both small and large mammals live in rain forests. The
100	jaguar is a rain forest mammal. It lives on the forest floor.
112	The sloth is a rain forest mammal. It does not live on the
125	forest floor. Sloths live in trees. They spend most of their
136	lives hanging upside down from tree branches.
143	There are many insects in a rain forest. They are
153	found in every layer. There are butterflies and beetles.
162	Worms and spiders live in rain forests. So do ants and
173	caterpillars.
174	Rain forests are home to millions of the earth's
183	animals and insects.
186	

Total Words Read _____

– Errors _____

= CWPM _____

Plants of the Rain Forest

0   Many kinds of plants grow in rain forests. They make

10   oxygen for the earth. Rain forest plants are used to make

21   medicine. Some of the plants can help stop cancer. Other

31   rain forest plants give us food. Passion flowers are rain

41   forest plants. People like to eat the fruit that grows on

52   these plants.

54   Liana vines are plants. They grow all over a rain

64   forest. The vines hook to each other. Animals swing on

74   liana vines to move from tree to tree.

82   Strangler fig trees grow in rain forests. This tree wraps

92   itself around other trees. It uses the other trees to grow

103   up to the sunlight. Then, the other trees die. Only the

114   strangler fig tree is left.

119   Orchids are plants with flowers. Orchid flowers grow

127   in many colors. They are very pretty. They grow in many

138   sizes and shapes.

141

Total Words Read _____

– Errors _____

= CWPM _____

Why Rain Forests Are Important

0	Tropical rain forests help the earth. They make almost
9	half of the world's oxygen. Rain forests may be the lungs
20	of our earth.
23	Rain forests help to work against global warming.
31	That means the earth is getting hotter. This is because
41	heat from the sun is trapped by gases in the air. Too much
54	carbon dioxide in the air makes it worse. Rain forest plants
65	take carbon dioxide from the air. They store it in their roots
77	and stems. They also store it in their leaves and branches.
88	Rain forests make up only 5% of the earth. But half of
100	the world's plants and animals live in them. Some of these
111	plants and animals are not found anywhere else on earth.
121	One-fourth of the medicines in the world come from rain
132	forest plants.
134	A lot of the world's food first came from rain forests.
145	Many nuts come from rain forests. So do fruits, like
155	bananas and pineapples. Lots of spices come from rain
164	forests, too.
166	

Total Words Read _____

− Errors _____

= CWPM _____

How We Can Help Save the Rain Forests

0	Many years ago, rain forests covered 20% of the earth.
10	Now, rain forests cover only 5% of the earth. Their trees
21	were cut down and sold for wood. One-and-a-half acres of
34	rain forest are lost every second.
40	Experts tell us that we must save the rain forests. They
51	are important to our earth. We need the rain forests. Once
62	the rain forests are gone, they will be gone forever. All of
74	the plants and animals that live there will be gone, too.
85	Everyone can help save the rain forests. There are
94	many things we can do. We can use less paper. Most
105	paper comes from trees. We can use less gas and plastic.
116	Gas and plastic are made from oil. The oil is taken from
128	rain forests. We can eat less red meat. Rain forests are cut
140	down to make room for cows. Cows are sold to make beef.
152	We should learn as much as we can about rain forests.
163	We can write letters to our leaders to ask for help in
175	saving the rain forests. We can raise money and give it to
187	programs that help rain forests. If people work together,
196	the rain forests can be saved.
202	

Total Words Read _____

– Errors _____

= CWPM _____

Level 3: The Human Body

Vocabulary

blood: A red liquid that the heart pumps throughout the body.

digest: To change food in the stomach into a form the body can use.

functions: Actions.

human: Relating to people.

muscles: Inside parts of a body that join bones together and make it possible for the body to move.

nerves: Thin parts (like threads) throughout the human body that help to control movement. Nerves work with the brain to send and receive messages of feelings like heat, cold, pain, etc.

skeletal: Having to do with a skeleton.

skeleton: The bone structure of the human body.

system: A set of related things that work together as a single unit.

The Human Body Introduction

0	People come in all sizes. Some are big. Some are
10	medium. Some are small. People have different skin color.
19	They have different hair color. People come in different
28	shapes.
29	No matter how they look, all people have the same
39	kind of body. All human bodies are exactly the same on
50	the inside.
52	Every body has the same parts. The parts are in
62	groups, which are called systems. The skeleton is one
71	system. It is made of hard bones. Muscles are another
81	system. Muscles make it possible for the body to move.
91	They are attached to the skeleton. The blood system has
101	arteries and veins. They carry blood to the other body
111	systems. Blood makes the other systems work. The brain
120	and the nervous system control how our bodies move. The
130	digestive system takes care of all food and drink.
139	The human body is an amazing machine!
146	

Total Words Read _____

− Errors _____

= CWPM _____

The Skeletal and Muscle System

0	Every human body has a skeleton made up of 206
10	bones. The skeleton supports the body. It gives the body
20	shape. It also protects the lungs and kidneys. Bones are
30	strong enough to support the body. They are also light
40	enough so that the body can move. Bones are made of
51	proteins. They are also made of minerals. Bone marrow is
61	inside the bone. This is where red blood cells are made.
72	Our bodies make more than one hundred million red blood
82	cells every day.
85	Muscles are fixed to the skeleton. A human body has
95	about 640 muscles. The muscles make the body move.
104	Muscles move all the time. Even when the body is still,
115	some muscles are still moving. They never stop working.
124	Muscles keep our lungs breathing. The heart is the most
134	important muscle. It keeps blood pumping throughout our
142	body.
143	

Total Words Read _____

– Errors _____

= CWPM _____

The Heart and Lung System

0   Every human body has blood flowing through it. The

9   body's blood never stops moving. It travels through a big

19   network of pipes. They are the veins and arteries.

28   Blood is made up of three different parts: red blood

38   cells, white blood cells, and platelets. These parts float in

48   a clear liquid called *plasma*. Red blood cells carry oxygen

58   throughout the body. White blood cells attack germs in the

68   body. Platelets stop the bleeding when we cut ourselves.

77   They help skin to heal.

82   The body needs oxygen to live. Oxygen keeps the

91   body working. When a person breathes, air goes into the

101   lungs. Lungs are like two big air bags. Inside the lungs

112   are tiny holes called *air sacs*. They are surrounded by tiny

123   blood channels. The heart pumps blood through them.

131   Oxygen goes through the air sacs and enters the blood.

141   The heart pumps this oxygen-rich blood through the

150   arteries. The blood is then returned to the heart and lungs

161   through the veins.

164

Total Words Read _____

– Errors _____

= CWPM _____

The Nervous System

0	The nervous system controls body functions. It is
8	made up of the brain, spinal cord, and many nerves. The
19	brain controls the body's five senses. They are the ability
29	to see, hear, feel, smell, and taste. The brain also controls
40	the body's parts so that they work well together.
49	The human brain is made up of many parts. The
59	largest part is the *cerebrum*. This is the thinking part of the
71	brain. The *cerebellum* is at the back of the brain. It controls
83	movement and balance. The *brain stem* is at the top of the
95	spinal cord. It connects the brain to the spinal cord. The
106	brain stem controls movements that keep the body alive.
115	These include breathing, digesting food, and the beating of
124	the heart.
126	The spinal cord runs up and down the neck and back
137	of your body. It is made up of nerves. When nerves are
149	grouped together, they carry messages. Sensory nerves
156	send messages to the brain. Motor nerves carry messages
165	from the brain to muscles to make them move. The
175	nervous system is the body's control center.
182	

Total Words Read _____

− Errors _____

= CWPM _____

The Digestive System

0	The digestive system takes care of the food we eat.
10	Every body needs food for fuel. Food gives the body
20	energy. It helps the body build new cells.
28	In order for food to turn into energy for the body, it
40	must be changed. That is the job of the digestive system. It
52	breaks down food and drink into their smallest parts. The
62	food is changed into nutrients. Nutrients can be absorbed
71	into the blood. The blood carries the nutrients to cells
81	throughout the body.
84	Digestion starts in the mouth. This is where food
93	and drink enter the body. The esophagus connects the
102	throat to the stomach. The esophagus moves food from
111	the throat. It pushes food down the neck and into the
122	stomach. The stomach is a mixer. It mashes all the food
133	together. Stomach acid turns the food into a liquid mixture.
143	Then it sends this mixture to the small intestine. The
153	small intestine breaks down the food even more. The liver,
163	pancreas, and gall bladder help with this job.
171	Leftover waste that the body can't use is sent on to
182	the large intestine. It stays there until it is expelled from
193	the body.
195	

Total Words Read _____

− Errors _____

= CWPM _____

Level 3: Holiday Celebrations

Vocabulary

celebrate: To take part in a special activity for a particular event.

custom: A common way of celebrating or recognizing an event.

holiday: A special day in honor of a custom or an event.

honor: To treat a person or an event with special respect.

special: Something that is more important than usual.

Holidays Introduction

0	Holidays are special days. They are days that are
9	important to us. They help us remember the past. Holidays
19	are times for people to celebrate. Many people do not have
30	to work on holidays. Schools may be closed.
38	Most countries have holidays. They also have
48	customs. A custom is a special way of doing something.
55	People celebrate their customs. They have fun with their
64	families. They have fun with their friends.
71	Many countries have the same holidays. Some
78	celebrate New Year's Day, the first day of the year. Some
89	countries celebrate Valentine's Day. It is a day to show
99	love. Some countries celebrate Independence Day. It is
107	their country's birthday. Thanksgiving is another holiday
114	in some countries. People give thanks for all of the good
125	things they have in their lives.
131	

Total Words Read _____

– Errors _____

= CWPM _____

New Year's Day

0	The first day of a new year is a holiday in many
12	countries. New Year's Day is a time to say good-bye to the
25	old year. It is a time to welcome the new year. People all
38	over the world celebrate New Year's in many ways.
47	In the U.S., New Year's Day is January 1. It is the first
60	day of the new calendar year. People celebrate by having
70	parties. They also watch parades and go to football games.
80	In Japan, New Year's Day is also January 1. Their
90	celebration lasts for three days. The date for the Chinese
100	New Year is different each year. Some years it starts in
111	January. In other years, it starts in February. The Chinese
121	celebration lasts for one month. The Jewish New Year
130	starts in either September or October. The celebration lasts
139	for ten days. It begins at sundown of the first day. It ends
152	at sundown of the last day.
158	People have been celebrating New Year's Day for
166	thousands of years. It is a time to reflect on the past and
179	look forward to the future.
184	

Total Words Read _____

− Errors _____

= CWPM _____

Valentine's Day

0	Valentine's Day may have been named after Saint
8	Valentine. He was a Christian priest who lived during
17	Roman times. In those days, many Christians were put
26	in jail just because of their religion. Valentine was one of
37	them. He would not change his religion. So he was killed
48	on February 14 in the year A.D. 269. He left a note to a
62	friend. He signed the note, "Your Valentine."
69	Today, many countries celebrate this holiday on
76	February 14. It is a day for people to show love. People
88	send cards to their sweethearts. They also send cards to
98	their friends and family.
102	In the U.S., it is the custom for men to give presents
114	to their sweethearts. The gifts are often candy or flowers.
124	Children celebrate Valentine's Day, too. They have parties
132	at school. They give cards to each other.
140	In Japan, women are the gift-givers. They give gifts to
151	men they like. If a Japanese man gets a gift, he must give a
165	gift in return one month later, on March 14.
174	In England, people bake treats for gifts. They make
183	Valentine buns with raisins or plums baked inside.
191	People all over the world enjoy Valentine's Day. No
200	matter what their custom, the day is all about love.
210	

Total Words Read _____

− Errors _____

= CWPM _____

Independence Day

0	Independence Day is a special day. It is the birth of a
12	country. It is a day of freedom. Many countries celebrate.
22	The 4th of July is a U.S. holiday. The U.S. became
33	a free country on that day in 1776. It became free from
45	British rule. People like to celebrate on July 4. Families get
56	together. They watch parades and wave flags. They also
65	have picnics with lots of food. Many people eat hot dogs.
76	They also eat watermelon. People watch fireworks after
84	dark. The beautiful colors light up the sky.
92	July 14 is a French holiday. It is Bastille Day. France
103	became a republic on that day in 1789. The French people
114	did not want to be ruled by a king. They decided that they
127	should rule themselves.
130	July 1 is a holiday in Canada. It is Canada Day. It is
143	their date of freedom. Britain gave Canada home rule on
153	that day in 1867.
157	

Total Words Read _____

- Errors _____

= CWPM _____

Thanksgiving Day

0	Thanksgiving is a special day. For years, people have
9	set aside one day to give thanks for gifts that the earth has
22	provided. Long ago, it was a time to honor the fall harvest.
34	Harvest is the time when crops are taken from the fields.
45	They were stored for the winter. People were thankful that
55	they had food to eat. They gave thanks for a good growing
67	season. All major religions give thanks for the earth's
76	bounty.
77	Thanksgiving is celebrated in the U.S. It is on the
87	fourth Thursday in November. Family and friends have a
96	big meal. They eat lots of turkey, stuffing, and cranberries.
106	There is pumpkin pie for dessert. Sometimes, people travel
115	many miles to share this meal.
121	Many people celebrate Thanksgiving in their own way.
129	It is a day to give thanks for life's blessings and fruits of
142	the earth.
144	

Total Words Read _____

− Errors _____

= CWPM _____

Level 3: Homes of the Past

Vocabulary

abundant: A great amount of.

bark: The outside covering of a tree.

covered: Wrapped around or spread over.

element: A part or piece of a whole.

frame: A series of parts that fit together to make a shape.

hide: An animal skin.

Native Americans: The first people to live on the land that became the United States of America.

natural resources: Things found in nature that are helpful to people.

Native Americans

0	Native Americans were the first people to live in the
10	United States. They settled in groups across the land. Each
20	group had its own language and customs. Customs are
29	special ways of doing things. Some groups shared the same
39	culture, or way of living. Language is a part of a culture.
51	So are the clothes that people wear and the food they eat.
63	A certain type of house is part of a culture, too.
74	Native Americans depended on nature to live. They
82	made good use of the natural resources. Natural resources
91	are things found in nature. They are useful to people.
101	Land is a natural resource. So are water and air. Fish and
113	animals are natural resources, too.
118	Native Americans used things from nature to build
126	their homes. People in the Northwest lived in lodges.
135	Those in the Southwest lived in pueblos. The Plains
144	people lived in tepees. People in the Northeast lived in
154	longhouses.
155	

Total Words Read _____

− Errors _____

= CWPM _____

Northwest Homes: Wood Lodges

0   Trees are a natural resource of the Northwest. The

9   Native Americans who lived there used trees to build their

19   homes. They lived in wood lodges. The lodges were long,

29   rectangular buildings. Each one was large enough for

37   several families.

39   The first step in building a lodge was to make a wood

51   frame. The frame was then covered with boards or tree

61   bark. Strips of bark were sewn together. Then the pieces

71   were attached to the frame.

76   Each lodge had one big room. It was dark inside

86   because lodges had no windows. In the middle of the

96   room was a fire pit for cooking. A hole in the roof above

109 the pit let the smoke outside. All of the families in a lodge

122 shared the fire pit. One area of the lodge was for sleeping.

134 Another area was for storing food and small items. Larger

144 items like boat paddles were stored outside the lodge.

153   Every lodge had a totem pole outside. The totem

162 pole was different for each lodge. A totem pole was an

173 important element of a lodge. It was a form of identity of

185 the families that lived in the lodge.

192

Total Words Read _____

– Errors _____

= CWPM _____

Southwest Homes: Pueblos

0	Native Americans in the Southwest lived in the desert.
9	They lived in homes called pueblos. The desert did not
19	have many trees. Rocks and clay were natural resources
28	in the desert. These settlers mixed clay mud with wild
38	grasses to create adobe. Then, they used adobe as a
48	building material.
50	To build their homes, Native Americans poured thick
58	adobe on the ground for a first floor. They let the adobe
70	dry for many days. Next, they made thick adobe blocks
80	and placed them in the sun to dry. Adobe blocks were then
92	used to frame and build the pueblos. Wood poles were
102	used for the roofs.
106	These Southwestern homes were built on top of tall,
115	flat mountains. Pueblos looked like apartment buildings.
122	The rooms were close together. Many families lived in a
132	set of rooms. As the families grew in number, more rooms
143	were added. Pueblos were very good homes for an area
153	with a dry, hot climate and very little rainfall.
162	

Total Words Read _____

− Errors _____

= CWPM _____

Plains Homes: Tepees

0	Buffalos were a natural resource on the plains. The
9	Plains people ate buffalo meat. They used buffalo hide for
19	clothing and boots. Spoons were made from buffalo horns.
28	Glue was made from buffalo hooves. No part of the buffalo
39	was wasted.
41	Hunting buffalo was a very important part of life for
51	the Plains people. Because they followed the buffalo, they
60	needed homes that could be moved easily. Their homes
69	were called tepees. The word *tepee* means "to dwell."
78	About 10 people could live in one tepee.
86	Spruce trees were also used to make tepees. The trees
96	were used to make long poles. The tops of the poles were
108	tied together. The bottoms were spread out on the ground.
118	Then, the poles were covered with animal hide. They were
128	fastened to the ground. The tepee was shaped like a cone.
139	It had a fire pit in the middle. Smoke went up and out the
153	opening at the top of the tepee.
160	Tepees were good homes for the Plains people. Tepees
169	were easy to take down and carry whenever the people
179	moved to follow the buffalo.
184	

Total Words Read _____

− Errors _____

= CWPM _____

© 2007 Sopris West Educational Services.

Northeast Homes: Longhouses

0	Native Americans in the Northeast used trees to build
9	their homes. These homes were called longhouses. They
17	were long and narrow with curved roofs. The people used
27	poles to make wood frames. They cut strips of bark from
38	birch trees and soaked it in water. This made the bark soft
50	and flat. The people used tree roots to sew the bark strips
62	together. They used the bark to cover the wood frames
72	of the longhouses. Many families lived together in one
81	longhouse.
82	The longhouses were built next to each other in
91	villages. The Native Americans used tall tree poles to build
101	high walls around the villages. The high walls kept them
111	safe from attacks. Their villages were built near water.
120	The Native Americans used water for drinking, cooking,
128	and growing crops. Corn was one of their crops. They also
139	planted beans and squash. The crops were picked in the
149	fall and stored to eat in the winter.
157	

Total Words Read _____

− Errors _____

= CWPM _____

Level 3: The Solar System

Vocabulary

moon: A natural satellite that travels around a planet.

orbit: To travel around in a circle.

planet: A large body that orbits the sun in the solar system.

rotate: To spin on a fixed object or position.

solar system: The sun, nine planets, moons, and objects in space.

The Solar System Introduction

0   The solar system is made up of the sun, nine planets,
11   and many moons. All but two of the planets have at least
23   one moon. Asteroids, meteoroids, and comets are part of
32   the solar system, too. The sun is the center of our solar
44   system. Earth orbits around the sun.

50   There are nine planets: four inner planets and five
59   outer planets. The inner planets orbit close to the sun.
69   They are called the "rocky planets." They are made up
79   mostly of rock. They have a few or no moons. The five
91   outer planets orbit far from the sun. Most of them are
102 made up of gases. All of the outer planets except one have
114 many moons.

116 Asteroids are a part of the solar system. They are
126 made up of rock. Some people call them the "minor
136 planets." Meteoroids are part of the solar system. They
145 are smaller than asteroids, about the size of a pebble. The
156 solar system includes comets. They are made up of gas,
166 ice, and dust. They have long, thin orbits. They warm up
177 as they go around the sun. Comets form heads and tails.
188 Their tails are made of dust and ice. They look like falling
200 stars in the sky.

204 The United States sends spacecraft to explore the solar
213 system. There is still much to learn about the sun, the
224 planets, and other objects in our solar system.
232

Total Words Read _____

− Errors _____

= CWPM _____

The Inner Planets

0   The four inner planets are Mercury, Venus, Earth,
8 and Mars. They are closest to the sun in the solar system.
20 These planets are also called the "rocky planets."

28   Mercury is the second-smallest planet. It is the closest
38 one to the sun. Mercury is about the same size as the
50 moon. It is the fastest moving planet.

57   Venus is the second planet from the sun. It is the
68 hottest planet in the solar system. Venus looks like Earth.
78 It is about the same size. Venus is called "the morning
89 star" or "the evening star." Venus can easily be seen at
100 dawn or at dusk.

104   Earth is the third planet from the sun. It is the
115 fifth-largest planet. It has one moon. Earth is the only
126 known planet on which there is life. Earth rotates on
136 an imaginary, or a pretend, line. This line is called an
147 axis. Earth leans, or tilts, on this axis. The tilting causes
158 different parts of the Earth to face the sun at different
169 times of the day and year. As a result, we have morning,
181 afternoon, and evening in a day as well as four seasons in
193 a year.

195   Mars is known as the "red planet." It is the fourth
206 planet in order from the sun and has two moons. It takes
218 687 days for Mars to orbit the sun. Like Earth, Mars has
230 seasons. Since it takes Mars longer to orbit the sun, its
241 seasons are longer.

244

Total Words Read _____

− Errors _____

= CWPM _____

The Outer Planets

0 The five outer planets are Jupiter, Saturn, Uranus,

8 Neptune, and Pluto. All except Pluto are huge, made up of

19 gases, and have many moons. These planets orbit far away

29 from the sun.

32 Jupiter, the largest planet, is the fifth planet from the

42 sun. Jupiter is known to have at least 39 moons. A great

54 red spot can be seen on Jupiter. The red spot is a big

67 storm. It takes Jupiter more than 84 years to orbit the sun.

79 Saturn is the sixth planet from the sun and the

89 second-largest. It is known for its many rings. These rings

100 are made of ice chunks and rock. Saturn has 21 moons. It

112 takes Saturn about 30 years to orbit the sun.

121 Uranus is the seventh planet from the sun. It is a

132 huge, icy planet with a blue color. Uranus is the third-

143 largest planet in the solar system. It has 22 known moons.

154 Neptune is the eighth planet from the sun and the

164 fourth-largest in the solar system. It is a giant, cold planet

176 with very strong winds. Neptune has 8 known moons.

185 Pluto is the smallest planet. It is the farthest from

195 the sun. Unlike the other outer planets, Pluto is rocky,

205 with only one moon. It is smaller than some of the other

217 planets' moons.

219

Total Words Read _____

– Errors _____

= CWPM _____

Asteroids and Meteoroids

0   Asteroids are stony objects in space. Most asteroids

8   are made up of rock. A few are made up of the metals

21   iron and nickel. Some are a combination of both rock and

32   metal. Asteroids came in all sizes. Most are small, but

42   some are very large.

46   Asteroids orbit the sun in groups. The groups are

55   called asteroid belts. The belts are between the orbits of

65   Mars and Jupiter. Asteroids are often called the "minor

74   planets."

75   There are other objects in space. Meteoroids also exist.

84   Most are made up of asteroids. They were created when

94   they crashed into each other. So, they are smaller than

104   asteroids. Most are the size of a pebble. They also orbit the

116   sun. Some orbit in a group. But others orbit alone. Some

127   flying spacecrafts have been hit by these hard, tiny objects.

137

Total Words Read _____

− Errors _____

= CWPM _____

Comets

0	Comets are small, icy objects in the Earth's solar
9	system. They are composed of three parts. Each comet has
19	a nucleus, a coma, and a tail.
26	The nucleus is the center of a comet. It is a small
38	mass made up of ice, gas, and dust. The comet's coma
49	surrounds its nucleus. The coma is made up of water
59	vapor, gases, and ammonia. These two parts make up a
69	comet's head.
71	The third part of a comet is its long tail. It is made
84	up of dust and ion gases. A comet's tail is its most visible
97	part. The tail is formed when the comet is near the sun.
109	The tail always points away from the sun because solar
119	winds push it away. When the comet is moving toward
129	the sun, the tail is behind the comet. When the comet is
141	moving away from the sun, the tail is in front of the comet.
154	Comets orbit the sun. Some comets get so close to the
165	sun that they crash into it. These comets are called "sun
176	grazers."
177	

Total Words Read _____

– Errors _____

= CWPM _____

Level 3: Take Care of Waste!

Vocabulary

environment: Everything around us (such as land, water, air, manmade things).

manage: To control or organize.

recycle: To make something new from something old.

unsafe: Dangerous, risky, or harmful.

toxic: Poisonous; something that can kill.

waste: Things that are thrown away or let into the environment.

The Three R's

0	Every day, people throw many things into the trash. A
10	big dump truck picks up the trash, or waste material, and
21	takes it away. But where does all of that waste go? Most
33	of it goes to a local dump called a landfill. This can cause
46	problems.
47	First, in many parts of the country there is not much
58	space left in landfills to put the waste. Second, some of the
70	waste is not safe. It could cause harm to the environment
81	and to people. There are many things we can do to help
93	manage waste and to help make the environment safe.
102	People can help with the waste problem. They need
111	to learn about the "Three R's." The R's stand for reduce,
122	recycle, and reuse. People should practice the three R's
131	every day. We can all help protect our environment.
140	

Total Words Read _____

− Errors _____

= CWPM _____

Reduce

0	Reduce means to make something smaller. It also
8	means to use less of something. There are many things
18	people can do to reduce waste.
24	First, we can buy less and use less. We should buy
35	only what we need and use all of what we buy. Buying
47	things in bulk can reduce waste. This means to buy things
58	in big containers. For example, buy a big box of cereal
69	instead of several small boxes. There will be less to throw
80	away. Buying in bulk is also cheaper.
87	Second, we should use fewer store bags. When we
96	buy one or two things at a store, we should carry them
108	out in our hands. Or, we can bring a reusable bag with us
121	to the store. We should use this bag to carry the items we
134	buy. We need to remember to take plastic and paper bags
145	we already have at home back to the grocery store. Most
156	stores have a big box near the front door to put bags for
169	reuse or recycling.
172	Finally, we can get rid of junk mail. Reducing paper
182	use will help reduce waste. There are toll-free phone
192	numbers printed on catalogs that are mailed to us. We
202	can call the catalog company and ask to be taken off
213	its mailing list. Reducing waste will help protect our
222	environment.
223	

Total Words Read _____

− Errors _____

= CWPM _____

Recycle

0   Recycle means to turn a used object into one for a
11   new use. The objects are put through a special process.
21   Then, they can be used again. If something can't be
31   reused, it can probably be recycled. Every day, people
40   throw away things. Most of these things should not be in
51   a waste bin. They can be recycled. Save things like soda
62   cans, glass jars, and paper.

67   Old paper can be recycled. It can be made into new
78   paper for books. Glass can be melted down and then made
89   into new glass items. Old soda cans can be made into new
101 soda cans. A plastic soda bottle can even be made into a T-
114 shirt! An old phone book can be used to make a new one.

127 Everyone should recycle. We should never throw out
135 anything that can be recycled or reused. Most cities have
145 recycling centers where people can take items. Sometimes,
153 people are paid for their items. Schools and homes may
163 have recycling bins. People put items in the bins. Then, a
174 truck picks up the bin items. They are taken to recycling
185 centers.

186 Taking the time to recycle can help protect our
195 environment.

196

Total Words Read _____

– Errors _____

= CWPM _____

Reuse

0   Reuse means to use something more than once or

9   to give it to someone who needs it. Reusing things is an

21   important way to manage waste. There are many items we

31   can reuse.

33   First, we can stop throwing away plastic. Plastic cups,

42   forks, spoons, knives, plates, and bags should be saved.

51   They can be washed and reused. We can save water

61   bottles and soda cups. Many stores will let people refill

71   their own cups. Not only will we be managing waste, we

82   will be saving money at the same time.

90   Second, we can be careful about paper use. Cloth

99   napkins are better to use than paper napkins. Not only

109   are they larger and stronger, they can be washed and used

120   for many years. Paper and cloth gift bags can be reused,

131   too. When we get wrapped gifts, we can carefully unwrap

141   them. Then, we can use the gift wrap paper again instead

152   of throwing it away. We should remember to take cloth

162   bags with us to the store. Then we won't have to choose

174   between paper or plastic.

178   Finally, we can try to fix things that break. That is

189   better than throwing them in the trash. Or, if we can't fix

201   them, we can give them away. There are places that fix

212   broken items and then give them away. If we decide to

223   buy something new like a sofa or a bike, we should sell or

236   give away the old one. That way, the items will end up in

249   someone's home and not in a landfill. Reusing items will

259   help protect our environment.

263

Total Words Read _____

- Errors _____

= CWPM _____

Be Safe With Waste

0	There are many things around the house that are
9	not safe to throw away. They are toxic. Toxic items have
20	poison. They harm the environment. They can hurt or
29	even kill plants, animals, or people.
35	Most homes have toxic items. Many of the items are
45	for cleaning. They usually can be found in the kitchen.
55	They can also be found in the bathroom. Oven and shower
66	cleaners can be harmful. So can furniture polish.
74	Many people do not like to have bugs in their homes.
85	So they keep products in the house to kill bugs like ants or
98	flies. The products are toxic. They are poisonous.
106	Painting supplies are also dangerous. They are made
114	of chemicals that can be toxic if they are inhaled or eaten.
126	Even glue and felt-tip markers can be harmful.
135	We need to be safe with waste. First, we must read
146	the labels on harmful items. We must follow the directions
156	carefully. Second, we should never throw toxic materials in
165	the trash. We must not pour them down the drain or onto
177	the ground. They could end up in our water supply.
187	Everyone must handle toxic items carefully. This will
195	help protect our environment.
199	

Total Words Read _____

– Errors _____

= CWPM _____

Appendix

Phonetic Elements Record Graph

STUDENT _____ PHONETIC ELEMENT_____

- Enter a date in the bottom row, and color that column bar up to the number of words the student read on that date.

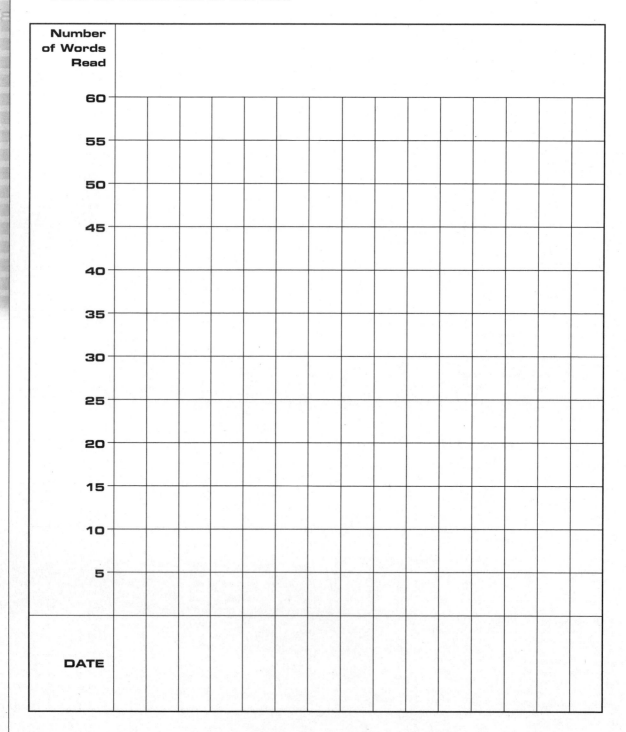

Automatic Words Record Graph

STUDENT _____ LIST # _____

- Enter a date in the bottom row, and color that column bar up to the number of words the student read on that date.

Number of Words Read

| 60 |
| 55 |
| 50 |
| 45 |
| 40 |
| 35 |
| 30 |
| 25 |
| 20 |
| 15 |
| 10 |
| 5 |
| DATE |

Initial Assessment Record (for passage reading)

TEACHER: _____

CLASS: _____ DATE: _____

- Rank students according to oral reading rate and then instructional reading level.

STUDENT NAME	ASSESSMENT 1—ORAL READING RATE (CWPM)	ASSESSMENT 2—INSTRUCTIONAL READING LEVEL

Parent Fluency Assessment Report

STUDENT _____

TEACHER _____ GRADE _____

EXPECTED CWPM FOR THIS GRADE LEVEL: _____

    Fluent reading is an important part of our language arts program. We will be assessing each student in this important reading skill during the school year.

    Please check your child's progress against the expected correct words per minute (CWPM) rate listed above as a measure of his/her progress in this vital skill.

Date	CWPM	Date	CWPM	Date	CWPM

Fluency Record

NAME: _____ CLASS: _____

PASSAGE NUMBER: _____

PARTNER: _____ DATE: _____

PASSAGE #	DATE	CWPM	DATE	CWPM	DATE	CWPM	DATE	CWPM	DATE	CWPM

CWPM = correct words per minute

Student Fluency Graph

NAME: _____ CLASS: _____

PARTNER: _____ DATE: _____

Correct Words Per Minute														
120														
115														
110														
105														
100														
95														
90														
85														
80														
75														
70														
65														
60														
55														
50														
45														
40														
35														
30														
25														
20														
15														
10														
5														
DATE														
FLUENCY SHEET NUMBER														
PASSAGE NUMBER														

Partner Points Sheet

PARTNER 1 NAME _____

PARTNER 2 NAME _____

- Mark one point for the partnership for each task done correctly.

Tasks	Date	Date	Date	Date	Date	Date	Date	Date
The materials were taken out quickly and quietly.								
Partner 1 and Partner 2 were ready to read at the right times.								
The partners helped each other to fix errors and record their scores.								
The materials were cleaned and put away quickly and quietly.								
TOTAL POINTS								

The ability to read text:

- Accurately

- Quickly

- With Expression

It is directly related to:

- Reading comprehension

- Independent reading

- Work completion

Bibliography

Adams, G., Brown, S., & Van Zant, S. (1999). Summer reading intervention program prepares fifth grade students for middle school reading challenges. *Educational Research Service Successful School Practices*, *22*(1), 6–8. Arlington, VA: Educational Research Service.

Adams, G., Brown, S., & Van Zant, S. (2000). Working with words: A summer reading intervention program. *Principal*, *80*(1), 59–60. Alexandria, VA: National Association of Elementary School Principals (NAESP).

Allington, R.L. (1977). If they don't read much, how are they ever gonna get good? *Journal of Reading*, *21*, 57–61.

Allington, R.L. (1983). Fluency: The neglected reading goal in reading instruction. *The Reading Teacher*, *36*, 556–561.

Archer, A.L., & Gleason, M.M. (2002). *Skills for school success series*. North Billerica, MA: Curriculum Associates, Inc.

Archer, A.L., Gleason, M.M., & Vachon, V.L. (2000). *REWARDS: Reading excellence, word attack, and rate development strategies*. Longmont, CO: Sopris West Educational Services.

Carnine, D., Silbert, J., & Kame'enui, E.J. (1997). *Direct instruction reading* (3rd ed.). Upper Saddle River, NJ: Prentice-Hall.

Carpenter, P.A., & Just, M.A. (1983). What your eyes do while your mind is reading. In K. Rayner (Ed.), *Eye movements in reading: Perceptual and language processes* (pp. 275–307). New York: Academic Press.

Carroll, J., Davies, P., & Richman, B. (1971). *The American heritage word frequency book*. Boston: Houghton Mifflin, American Heritage Publishing.

Consortium on Reading Excellence (CORE). (1999). *Assessing reading: Multiple measures*. Novato, CA: Arena Press.

Cunningham, A.E., & Stanovich, K.E. (1998). What reading does for the mind. *American Educator*, *22*(1–2), 8–15.

Cunningham, P. (2000). *Phonics they use*. Longman, NY: Addison Wesley.

Dowhower, S.L. (1987). Effects of repeated reading on second-grade transitional readers' fluency and comprehension. *Reading Research Quarterly*, *22*, 389–406.

Dowhower, S.L. (1994). Repeated reading revisited: Research into practice. *Reading and Writing Quarterly*, *10*, 343–358.

Farstrup, A.E., & Samuels, S.J. (Eds.). (2002). *What research has to say about reading instruction* (3rd ed.). Newark, DE: International Reading Association.

Foorman, B.R., & Mehta, P. (2002, November). *Definitions of fluency: Conceptual and methodological challenges*. PowerPoint® presentation at A Focus on Fluency forum, San Francisco, CA.

Fuchs, L.S., Fuchs, D., Kazlan, S., & Allen, S. (1999). Effects of peer-assisted learning strategies in reading with and without training in elaborated help giving. *Elementary School Journal*, *99*(3), 201–220.

Good, R.H., & Kaminski, R.A. (2003). *DIBELS: Dynamic indicators of basic early literacy skills*. Longmont, CO: Sopris West Educational Services.

Greenwood, C.R., Delquadri, J.C., & Hall, R.V. (1989). Longitudinal effects of classwide peer tutoring. *Journal of Educational Psychology*, *81*, 371–383.

Harcourt, Inc. (2001). Stanford achievement test series (9th ed.) (SAT-9). San Antonio, TX: Author.

Hasbrouck, J.E., & Tindal, G.A. (2005). *Oral reading fluency: 90 years of measurement* (Tech. Rep. No. 33, Behavioral Research and Teaching [BRT]). Eugene: University of Oregon, College of Education.

Hasbrouck, J. E., & Tindal, G.A. (in press). Oral reading fluency norms: A valuable assessment tool for reading teachers. *The Reading Teacher*.

Hudson, R.F., Lane, H.B., & Pullen, P.C. (2005). Reading fluency assessment and instruction: What, why, and how? *The Reading Teacher, 58*(8), 702–714.

Johns, J.L., & Lenski, S.D. (2001). Improving reading: A handbook of strategies (2nd ed., p. 164). Dubuque, IA: Kendall/Hunt Publishing Co.

Karlsen, B., & Gardner, E.F. (1995). *Stanford diagnostic reading test* (4th ed.). San Antonio, TX: Harcourt, Inc.

LaBerge, D., & Samuels, S.J. (1974). Toward a theory of automatic information processing in reading. *Cognitive Psychology, 6*, 293–323.

La Pray, M., Ross, H., & Ramon, R. (1969 January). The graded word list: Quick gauge of reading ability. *Journal of Reading, 12*(4), 305–307.

Levy, B.A. (2001). Moving the bottom: Improving reading fluency. In M. Wolf (Ed.), *Dyslexia, fluency, and the brain* (pp. 357–379). Timonium, MD: York Press.

Levy, B.A., Nicholls, A., & Kroshen, D. (1993). Repeated readings: Process benefits for good and poor readers. *Journal of Experimental Child Psychology, 56*, 303–327.

MacGinitie, W., MacGinitie, R., Maria, K., & Dreyer, L. (2003). *Gates-MacGinitie reading tests*. Itasca, IL: Riverside Publishing.

Mercer, C.D., Campbell, K.U., Miller, M.D., Mercer, K.D., & Lane, H.B. (2001). Effects of a reading fluency intervention for middle schoolers with specific learning disabilities. *Learning Disabilities Research and Practice, 15*, 179–189.

Meyer, M.S., & Felton, R.H. (1999). Repeated reading to enhanced fluency: Old approaches and new directions. *Annals of Dyslexia, 49*, 263–306.

Moats, L.C. (2001, March). When older kids can't read. *Educational Leadership Report*.

National Institute of Child Health and Human Development (NICHD). (2000). Report of the National Reading Panel: *Teaching children to read: An evidence based assessment of the scientific research literature on reading and its implications for reading instruction. Chapter 3: Fluency* (NIH Publication No. 00-4754). Washington, DC: U.S. Government Printing Office.

Pinnell, G.S., Piluski, J.J., Wixson, K.K., Campbell, J.R., Gough, P.B., & Beatty, A.S. (1995). *Listening to children read aloud: Data from NAEP's integrated reading performance record (IRPR) at grade 4* (Report No. 23–FR–04). Washington, DC: U.S. Department of Education, National Center for Education Statistics, Office of Educational Research and Improvement.

Rosenshine, B., & Meister, C. (1994). Reciprocal teaching: A review of research. *Review of Educational Research, 64*, 479–530.

Samuels, S.J. (1979). The method of repeated readings. *The Reading Teacher, 32*, 403–408.

Scholastic, Inc. (2003). *Scholastic reading inventory (SRI)*. New York: Author.

Shapiro, E.S. (1996). *Academic skills problems: Direct assessment and intervention* (2nd ed.). New York: Guilford Press.

Stanovich, K.E. (1986). Matthew effects in reading: Some consequences of individual differences in the acquisition of literacy. *Reading Research Quarterly, 21*, 360–407.

Stanovich, K.E. (1990). Concepts in developmental theories of reading skill: Cognitive resources, automaticity, and modularity. *Developmental Review, 10*, 72–100.

Stevens, R.J., Madden, N.A., Slavin, R.E., & Famish, A.M. (1987). Cooperative integrated reading and composition: Two field experiments. *Reading Research Quarterly, 22*, 433–454.

Stieglitz, E. (2002). *Stieglitz informal reading inventory: Assessing reading behaviors from emergent to advanced levels*. Boston: Allyn & Bacon.

Topping, K. (1987). Paired reading: A powerful technique for parent use. *The Reading Teacher, 40*, 608–614.

Torgesen, J.K., Rashotte, C.A., & Alexander, A. (2001). Principles of fluency instruction in reading: Relationships with established empirical outcomes. In M. Wolf (Ed.), *Dyslexia, fluency, and the brain* (pp. 333–355). Timonium, MD: York Press.

Wolf, M. (2001). *Dyslexia, fluency, and the brain*. Timonium, MD: York Press.

Woodcock, R.W. (2000). *Woodcock reading mastery test*. Circle Pines, MN: American Guidance Service.